DREADNOUGHT BATTLESHIP

Dreadnought and super dreadnought (1906–16)

COVER IMAGE: HMS *Dreadnought*. *(Alex Pang)*

First published in May 2016

A catalogue record for this book is available from the British Library.

ISBN 978 1 78521 068 6

Library of Congress control no. 2015948105

Copy editor: Michelle Tilling
Proof reader: Penny Housden
Indexer: Peter Nicholson
Design and layout: James Robertson

Published by Haynes Publishing,
Sparkford, Yeovil,
Somerset BA22 7JJ, UK.
Tel: 01963 440635
Int. tel: +44 1963 440635
Website: www.haynes.co.uk

Haynes North America Inc.,
861 Lawrence Drive, Newbury Park,
California 91320, USA.

Printed in the USA by Odcombe Press LP,
1299 Bridgestone Parkway, La Vergne,
TN 37086.

Acknowledgements

The author would like to thank the following people for their help and assistance during the writing and production of this book: from the HMS *Caroline* restoration team, Jonathan Porter and Billy Hughes for giving me interviews and for showing me around the ship; Jef Maytom for providing me with additional photographs of HMS *Caroline*; Stephen Courtney and Heather Johnson of the National Museum of the Royal Navy, who helped me to uncover invaluable archive sources and photographic material; Michelle Tilling at Bourchier for editing the material so diligently; and finally Jonathan Falconer of Haynes Publishing, for his continual support during the writing and production process.

DREADNOUGHT BATTLESHIP

Haynes

THE NATIONAL MUSEUM | ROYAL NAVY

Dreadnought and super dreadnought (1906–16)

Owners' Workshop Manual

Insights into the design, construction, operation and combat history of these revolutionary big-gun iron-clad battleships

Chris McNab

Contents

OPPOSITE C-class light cruiser HMS *Caroline*, the last survivor of the Battle of Jutland, is seen here while under restoration at Belfast in 2015. At her best rate of knots she could manage a speed of 28½kts. *(Jef Maytom)*

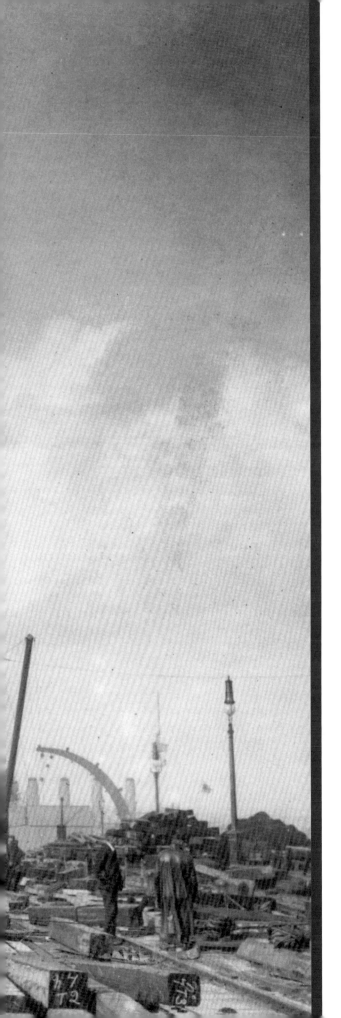

Chapter One

Dreadnoughts and super dreadnoughts – origins and evolution

The launch and commissioning of HMS *Dreadnought* in 1906 drew a line in the sand for the world's navies. At a stroke this revolutionary new warship seemed to occupy a new naval superiority, arguably rendering all other battleships obsolete and sparking an energetic international naval arms race.

OPPOSITE HMS *Dreadnought* in dock in 1906. Total costs for the manufacture of *Dreadnought* were £1,783,883 – an extraordinary amount at 1906/7 prices. *(National Museum of the Royal Navy – NMRN)*

At the turn of the 20th century, the Royal Navy reigned supreme over the world's oceans. Between 1901 and 1904, for example, the Navy boasted no fewer than 45 full-sized battleships in operation, the cream of its fleet, and three in reserve; this force alone a living testimony to British might in gun and steel. Furthermore, British industrial capacity was at its peak, the shipyards launching ships at a rate against which other nations could not compete. Hence in Europe in 1904 alone Germany laid down, launched or completed 24 battleships, France 17 and Russia 22. Britain, meanwhile, flexed its muscles by producing 39 warships – an astonishing output.

And yet, times were changing. New understanding of the development of naval warfare – as well as lessons learned from recent conflicts – were prompting some forward-looking individuals to seek a dramatic change in the primary tools of seaborne battle. Britain's venerable Royal Navy was about to undergo a seismic shift, one that would drag the rest of the world along in its wake.

The battleship arena

In the first years of the 20th century, the supreme expression of naval might was the battleship. Battleships had evolved from the wooden-hulled, steam-and-sail-powered vessels with smoothbore cannon typical of the mid-19th century, through to iron-hulled, armoured warships fitted with turreted breech-loading and rifled guns, driven by powerful steam engines. A typical example of such a beast was the British vessel *Irresistible*, one of the three battleships in the *Formidable* class. Laid down in April 1898 and completed in February 1902, the *Irresistible* was 431ft 8in long and had a displacement of 15,000 tons. Power came from two 3-cylinder vertical triple-expansion engines, fuelled by 20 Bellville-type water-tube boilers, with the related coal bunkers holding anywhere from 900 to 2,200 tons of coal. Maximum speed was 18 knots (21mph). The warship was wrapped in some hefty armour – at its shallowest on the main deck at 1in, while bulkhead and barbette armour could thicken up to 12in.

Most relevant to our emerging discussion was its armament. The armament of the 'pre-dreadnought' battleships was decidedly mixed, the warship designers covering all their tactical bases with firepower ranging downwards from hefty long-range 12in (sometimes 13in) guns down to diminutive deck guns used for close-range work. Thus the *Irresistible* had 4 × 12in 40-calibre Armstrong Whitworth main guns, set in pairs in turrets fore and aft; 12 × 6in Quick-Firing (QF) guns; 16 × 12-pdr QFs; 6 × 3-pdr guns; 4 × 18in torpedo tubes; and two machine guns for good measure.

The mixed armament of the pre-dreadnoughts was partly the result of the inadequacies of fire control rather than any mistrust in the capabilities of the individual gun sets. Accurate naval gunnery at range was still rather in its infancy, and while the heaviest guns had capabilities of up to some 15,000yd, the limitations of fire control meant that the typical maximum combat range was just 2,000yd. Hence having batteries of smaller guns was a useful insurance policy in case the combat closed quickly to shorter ranges; the more nimble, quick-firing guns – so the thinking went – would be able to smother the target with sheer weight of shot, while the big guns became more cumbersome and less effective against more proximate targets. The lighter guns could also respond more quickly to small, fast attackers. This was not to say that the issue of the correct distribution and weight of firepower was a done deal. In fact, it inspired passionate debate, and opting for a mixed argument was one way to bypass all the arguments and hedge your bets.

The all-big-gun battleship

The figure who dominated the early stages of dreadnought development is John Fisher (1841–1920), one of the landmark figures in the history of the modern Royal Navy. By the turn of the 20th century, Fisher had already been in the Navy an astonishing 46 years (he had entered the service in 1854 at the age of 13). Fisher was appointed First Sea Lord in 1904, a position he held until 1910. During this time, his administrative and organisational vision, plus his deep understanding of the principles and technologies of naval gunnery, helped revolutionise warship design.

With Fisher's ascent to First Sea Lord, he plunged himself into the debate already hinted at – the best design for the Navy's capital ships. Essentially, the fire of the debate burned upon two main issues – speed and gunnery. Regarding the tactical merits of speed, there were those who argued that speed was a relative affair, essentially unimportant if the enemy was achieving the same speeds as your own ships. But tactical lessons, especially from the Russo-Japanese War, showed that

LEFT Admiral John Arbuthnot 'Jackie' Fisher, the man whose commitment to the dreadnought vision led to a reshaping of global naval power at the start of the 20th century.

speed remained a critical factor in both the manoeuvre to advantageous gunnery positions and the ability to get out of trouble. The steady improvement of steam power since its first applications to seagoing vessels in the early 19th century meant that vessels were becoming steadily faster. New engine types were also being introduced, the most relevant to our discussion being the steam turbine, first set aboard the steamship *Turbinia* in 1894.

Turbines offered a range of advantages over the traditional reciprocating types. They were in many ways mechanically simpler and therefore more reliable, and also cleaner to run; in addition, these qualities meant that they were generally cheaper both to build and operate. They could be made lighter and smaller than equivalent power reciprocating types. These factors had key benefits for warship design, not least that the powerplant could be fitted into a small space on the ship (the space savings being valuable for other purposes), plus the lower profile meant that more of the engine

BELOW Launched on 2 August 1894, the *Turbinia* was the first steam turbine-powered steamship, built as a proof of concept for the Royal Navy. *Turbinia* revealed issues with turbine technology, such as propeller cavitation.

could be located down below the waterline, protected from gunfire by the sea and belt armour. Turbines also offered greater fuel economy at high speeds, meaning turbine-powered ships had better endurance in combat operations.

Yet during the early 20th century, turbines were still very much in their infancy, and they had a fair set of problems. Chief among these was that the performance characteristics of turbines were best expressed at high speeds; at cruising speeds and during lower-powered manoeuvres, they were actually not as efficient, and could give a vessel handling problems. Furthermore, prior to 1906, in the Royal Navy turbines had only been applied to a small handful of vessels, chiefly destroyers – they had not been tested within the context of a major battleship. Essentially the turbine was unproven in a capital ship. Also allied to the question of speed was that of the levels of armour applied to the ship. Increase the weight of armour and you decrease the speed, and vice versa – the appropriate equation between the two was the source of a river of military academic papers and debates.

But of even greater focus for the naval community was the issue of gunnery – its composition, type and control. As we have already seen, the battleships of the first years of the 20th century had a mixed selection of armament, the core of the naval weaponry being a main armament of 4 × 12in guns plus a secondary armament of 12 × 6in guns. In 1906, however, the launch of the dreadnought type saw a switch to an 'all-big-gun'

arrangement of 10 × 12in guns. This did not mean that there was no secondary armament – indeed the *Dreadnought* had a large number of additional guns. Yet the secondary armament was of reduced range and firepower compared to that of the previous vessels; the main ship-killing duties were now firmly in the hands of the big guns. So what prompted Fisher, and other like-minded individuals, to pursue this shift?

There were essentially three considerations behind this change – threats, fire control and experience. Taking the threats first, Fisher became increasingly concerned about the capabilities of torpedo warfare. Although the first torpedoes of the 19th century had a very limited range, by 1904 naval authorities were receiving reports that effective ranges of these weapons had now increased to around 3,000yd. By the following year, the range was extended to around 4,500yd. Although the torpedoes were inaccurate, they could be fired in 'spreads' of multiple weapons, to increase the likelihood of a hit. During the Russo-Japanese War (1904–5), a battleship, two cruisers and two destroyers were sunk by torpedoes. The lesson for Fisher was clear: soon torpedoes would outrange gunfire, and thus the capital vessels had to be capable of engaging targets accurately at long ranges. This was the job of the big guns.

The word 'accurately' was key here, and therein lay that problem. As noted above, around the 1890s the maximum range of the effective gunfire was classed as being about 2,000yd. However, from 1898 the British Mediterranean Fleet began long-range gunnery trials, experimenting with new methods of extending the engagement range. The distances were stretched by the combination of 'spotting' – observers watching the fall of shot and providing the gun crews with elevation and traverse adjustments on to target – plus improved rangefinder technologies. (More about the technicalities of gunnery will be explored in Chapter 3.) Through practice and technical advance, the ranges reached out inexorably, so that by 1904 initial engagement ranges of 10,000yd were considered possible, although the effective range was more in the region of 8,000yd.

BELOW *Navarin* was a pre-dreadnought Russian battleship. Launched on 20 October 1891, *Navarin* was lost to mines during the Battle of Tsushima in May 1905.

Bearing this in mind, a bold question mark suddenly hung over the shorter-range secondary armament. Thinkers such as Fisher and the influential Sir Philip Watts, from 1902 the Director of Naval Construction (DNC), began to feel that it was better to have the armament stacked in favour of the big guns, which could decide the battle at long range. To clarify this point further, it is useful to quote from a significant contemporary of Fisher, the great Earl John Jellicoe (1859–1935), who between 1905 and 1908 was the Navy's Director of Naval Ordnance. In *Considerations of the Design of a Battleship*, written in 1906 when the *Dreadnought* development programme was under way, he observed:

The recent development of the prospect of hitting frequently at long ranges is the all-important fact which has brought the value of the heaviest gun prominently forward, and which culminates in the design of the 'Dreadnought.' Fire effect at any range is the product of the number of hits in a given time (intensity of hitting) and the effect of the individual hit. [...]

Now by reason of its flatter trajectory the big gun is easier to hit with at long ranges than is the smaller, and the larger the gun the greater is the comparative as well as the actual effect of the individual hit. So far as the rate of firing of the bigger gun is less than that of the smaller calibres,

the number of hits may be expected to be less, but by no means proportionate to the lower rate of fire, as its superior flatness of trajectory not only produces a larger proportion of hits to rounds fired but further the smaller gun can never at long ranges attain a rate of fire approaching in any degree to the maximum possible owing firstly to the necessity of observation of the effect of the firing if such firing is to be effective in the least degree, and secondly to the fact that the quantity of smoke produced by the rapid fire of a number of small guns effectually prevents the effects of the fire being observed and thus automatically reduces the rate of fire.

Jellicoe, Considerations of the
Design of a Battleship, *1906*

ABOVE *King Edward VII* emerged on to the world scene with unfortunate timing. This powerful pre-dreadnought was commissioned in 1905, but a year later she was technically obsolete. The ship was sunk by a mine in 1916. *(LOC)*

BELOW A port-side view of one of *King Edward VII*'s BL 9.2in secondary armament. *Dreadnought* questioned the rationale of such weapons. *(LOC)*

Jellicoe's argument is simple – the big guns might realise fewer overall hits in relation to the smaller guns, but the flatter trajectory of the weapons (which makes fire adjustment easier) means that they can achieve a proportionately greater number of strikes per shells fired. Furthermore, the destructive effect of the big shells was little short of awesome; a single well-placed or fortuitous hit from a 12in shell could take out an entire warship. There is the additional point that when shells were falling around an enemy ship, it was hard for the observers to tell the calibre from the water splash, thereby causing problems for giving adjustment instructions to individual batteries. If the fire exchange was conducted by batteries of uniform calibre, then telling which shell came from which battery was not especially important.

So, the threat of torpedoes plus improvements in gunnery and fire control were two influences that fuelled Fisher, Watts, Jellicoe and sympathetic others to look towards a new generation of warships. Plus there was the added impetus given by experience. The Western naval community looked on with notebooks in hand as the Russo-Japanese War brought two well-developed navies – both armed with turreted battleships, cruisers and other modern vessels – into open conflict. The advantage that Japan took in battles such as the epic clash at Tsushima on 27 May 1905, in which the Russians suffered catastrophic losses of 20 ships sunk and 6 captured, was largely due to their forward-thinking commitment to sound training, more judicious choice of ammunition and their investment in the British Barr and Stroud FA3 coincidence rangefinder. Significantly, the big-gun exchanges began at about 7,000yd, illustrating that the days of the 2,000yd clash were long gone. In other engagements during the conflict, shells were even fired at extreme ranges of 17,000yd.

Fisher was highly aware that other nations were also starting to reflect upon the potential advantages of the all-big-gun battleship. Even back at the end of the 19th century, British strategists were becoming aware that the

LEFT Pre-dreadnought HMS *Commonwealth* was part of the *King Edward VII* class, known as the 'wobbly eight' because of their short period of roll.

seemingly unassailable superiority of British naval power was by no means etched in stone. For a start, there were now more players on the field. While for much of the 19th century only France and Russia were equal contenders to British naval might, in the last two decades of the century the United States, Germany and Japan all began to develop battle fleets centred around cruisers and battleships. The American efforts, led by figures such as US Secretaries of the Navy Benjamin Tracy then Hilary Herbert, plus the legendary naval strategist Alfred Thayer Mahan, were at first treated rather condescendingly by the British, but started to flatten the smirks once substantial warships began to emerge with regularity.

Germany initiated its warship building in earnest in the 1870s and 1880s, at first concentrating principally on cruisers and torpedo boats, but laying down a new series of battleships from 1883. Under the leadership of Admiral Alfred von Tirpitz, Secretary of State of the Ministry of Marine from 1897 to 1916, the German Navy entered a fresh era of warship building, showing genuine aspirations to compete with Britain on the high seas. Fisher would have also been very aware of the 1903 article by Italian naval expert Vittorio Cuniberti in *Jane's Fighting Ships*. The article was pertinently titled 'An ideal battleship for the British Navy'. This ideal warship in question

was to have a 17,000-ton displacement and an armament of 12 × 12in guns. Armour protection was to be a maximum of 12in and the ship would have a top speed of 20 knots. Fisher was likely aware that if he didn't respond to such prescient visions, others would.

A technological naval arms race was emerging, with each side looking for the next advantage. The concept of a warship dominated by a single heavy gun armament was not a British possession alone, and Fisher became aware that the clock was ticking.

LEFT The *Kaiser Barbarossa* was a classic German pre-dreadnought, part of the *Kaiser Friedrich III* class of battleships. Note how the turreted 9.2in guns are mounted above the 5.9in secondary armament. *(LOC)*

The dreadnought emerges

Fisher's journey into battleship redesign began in about 1903. He was not acting alone; indeed he was to a large extent following the lead of Sir Philip Watts, who laboured over a vision for a turbine-powered, heavily armoured warship with turreted heavy armament. Other individuals helping him to channel his thoughts included naval architects John Harper Narbeth and Henry Deadman; Alexander Gracie, who was Managing Director of the Fairfield Shipbuilding Company; W.H. Gard, the Chief Constructor of Portsmouth Dockyard; and three intelligent captains, Bacon, Madden and Jackson. Debate was lively, particularly about the composition and calibre of the ship's guns. In October 1904, Fisher had narrowed his thoughts down to two basic ship formats, both of 16,000 tons displacement and with similar levels of performance. One type was proposed with a main armament of 16 × 10in guns, while the other had 8 × 12in guns. The decision fell in favour of the 12in guns, but then came the vexing questions of how many guns and how should they be located and configured around the ship? The designers had to ensure that the ship had the optimal capability for both broadship and end-on fire. The process of choosing this warship design was given additional authority by the formation of a sympathetic Committee on Design in October 1904, composed of an august panel of naval experts from all branches of the service.

The various designs, given letters of the alphabet, ground their way through the committee evaluation, but eventually, on 18 January 1905, Design 'H' became the accepted format. A basic description of the battleship, to be called HMS *Dreadnought*, gives us a sense of what was about to emerge on to the high seas. *Dreadnought* was to have a length of 526ft overall, and a beam of 82ft. The armour had a depth of 11–4in around the belt, the same around the barbettes, 11in on the gun shields and conning tower, 8in on the bulkheads and signal tower, and between 1.75 and 3in on the three decks. The complement

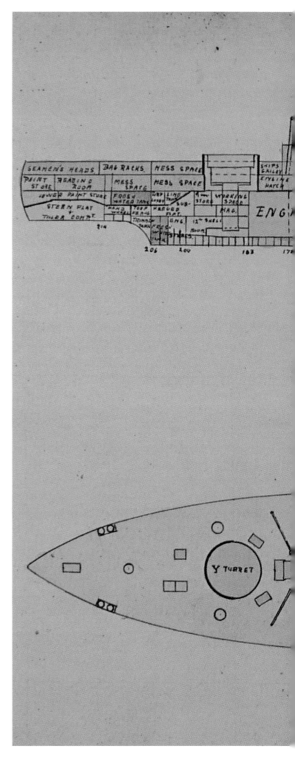

was to be 675 men. Performance, delivered via turbine technology generating 23,000shp, was a maximum speed of 21 knots.

When it came to the critical, indeed defining, issue of the ship's armament, the warship's main armament was provided in the form of 10 × 12in guns. These were arranged in twin

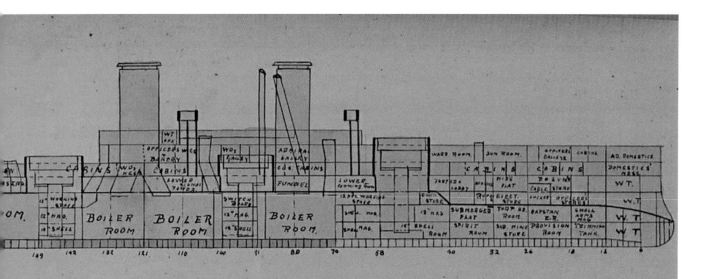

PROFILE.

H.M.S. DREADNOUGHT.

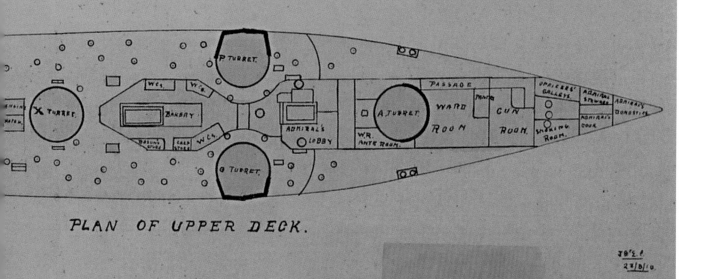

PLAN OF UPPER DECK.

turrets as follows: three turrets were set on the centreline – one fore, one aft and one amidships – and there was another turret on each beam. Bearing in mind that the wing turrets could also be presented to fire forward, the total fire profile was six guns to the front, eight to each broadside, and six to the rear. Apart from the main guns, the *Dreadnought* was also to be equipped with a secondary anti-torpedo boat armament of 18 × 12-pdrs, while for making torpedo attacks herself the ship had five torpedo tubes below the waterline. (More about the detailed layout of the ship will be explained in Chapter 2.)

ABOVE A plan of HMS *Dreadnought* as built. Note the positioning of the 'P' and 'Q' wing turrets, with their necessarily limited traverse. *(NMRN)*

LEFT A forward view of *Dreadnought* under construction in 1906. Note the shape of the bow, with its C-profile designed to reduce the severity of the bow wave. *(NMRN)*

CENTRE Another view of the *Dreadnought* hull on the ways, this time looking from the stern. *(NMRN)*

With the *Dreadnought* design finalised and approved by the Committee and by the Admiralty, all that now remained was for the ship to be built. Speed was of the essence. The Admiralty was aware that as soon as the ship's properties and qualities were revealed to the global naval community, Britain would be in a race to stay ahead, hence the ship had to go from keel-laying to commission in record time. This goal was indeed achieved, through the spectacular efforts of Thomas Mitchell, the Manager Constructive Department (MCD), plus what would eventually be a total construction workforce of 3,000 men, labouring virtually around the clock. The timings were consequently truly impressive, even in the context of the greatest shipbuilding nation in the world at that time.

The keel was laid down in Portsmouth Dockyard on 2 October 1905 and the ship was launched, with King Edward VII performing

RIGHT Here *Dreadnought* is undergoing the fitting-out process. Note the rotating mechanisms of 'Y' and 'X' turret for traversing the twin 12in guns. *(NMRN)*

the ceremony, on 10 February 1906. On 29 September she received her crew, conducted steam trials over the following two weeks, and a 24-hour acceptance trial on 1–2 December. On 11 December, the new warship became part of the Special Service Home Fleet, and took her full complement of crew. The very next month, *Dreadnought* began a three-month experimental cruise, and was fully revealed to an expectant world.

Countering criticisms

Any radically different weapon system attracts criticism, and the *Dreadnought* was no exception. The *Dreadnought* seemed to polarise opinion around the world. There were those who regarded the vessel as a triumphant revolution in naval design – one that gave the Royal Navy a formidable lead in the naval arms race. It is common in books and articles on the *Dreadnought* and the dreadnought class to say that the warship rendered all other battleships obsolete. We need to be precise in what we mean by this. Essentially, the advocates of the *Dreadnought* believed that such warships would be able to outgun their opponents at long ranges, effectively destroying them through thunderous weight of 12in fire before they had the chance to bring their own guns or torpedoes to bear. The dreadnoughts would also have the speed to perform rapid battle manoeuvres and deployments, faster than foreign ships of equivalent size, and would have the armour to survive battering shellfire exchanges.

Yet far from everyone was convinced. American authorities such as Thayer were unimpressed, saying that the slower-firing, heavier guns of the *Dreadnought* would leave it open to being overwhelmed by the more rapid-firing secondary armament of other warships at closer ranges. Sir William Henry White, Chief Constructor of the Admiralty, gave a lecture at the Society of Arts on 12 February 1906, two days after *Dreadnought*'s launch, in which he expressed his reservations publicly. *The Times* reported his views as follows:

The practical abolition of the secondary armament was no new idea and had been a subject of discussion for years; it was really a tendency to return to the state of things that existed in the old DREADNOUGHT, which had four heavy guns and nothing else but very light guns. The argument was that with the very long ranges now unavoidable no gun but the 12in. was worth having; therefore the proper course was to get rid of all the others, with the concurrent advantage of simplifying the ammunition supply. On the other hand, it was an unproved assumption that the 12in. was the only gun worth considering. That penetration was not the only thing shown in the late war, when the Russians declared they were blinded by the Japanese fire from smaller guns. To suggest that one ship with ten 12in. guns would be equal to two or three earlier battleships each carrying four 12in. guns was another unproved assumption. To judge from published descriptions of the DREADNOUGHT, she had two 12in. guns in a forecastle, with two pairs of the same guns behind; in that case, in the conditions that would give six guns ahead, continuous sighting would be impossible for four of them. Again, the ammunition for these six guns must be massed in a comparatively small longitudinal area. He did not wish to raise objections to the DREADNOUGHT but from what had been published about her it appeared that the desire to increase bow fire and broadside fire it involved serious drawbacks and left untouched the objections to the omission of a secondary armament.

The Times, 13 February 1906

This was just the tip of the iceberg when it came to the criticisms. They were assailed for being too expensive, not manoeuvrable enough, of unproven reliability and vulnerable to attack. An examination of the primary sources from this period reveals numerous Admiralty documents defending the *Dreadnought* from its detractors. Publicly, the Admiralty was rather hamstrung in its defence, because they wanted to play down the revolutionary nature of the design to allow them to build up a construction lead over competing nations. Behind closed doors, however, Fisher and his associates could be more robust. The Admiralty Board document entitled *H.M. Ships 'Dreadnought' and 'Invincible'* and labelled 'Strictly Secret', is typical, and is quoted at length here.

The features of these novel designs which have been most adversely criticised are:

1. The uniform 12-inch armament.
2. The increase in speed.
3. The increase in size and cost due to 1 and 2.

1. *The Armament*. – The papers by the Controller and Director of Naval Ordnance deal with the reasons which led to the adoption of the uniform 12-inch armament argued from the constructors' and gunnery points of view and prove the wisdom of the Admiralty policy of adopting a uniform armament of the heaviest gun in use. A very convincing argument will also be found in the following statement, which is based on the average of the results obtained by the Fleet in the 1905 battle practice: it shows the weight of projectiles in pounds that would hit an enemy (the size of the practice battle target) in 10 minutes if the rapidity and accuracy of fire from a pair of 6-inch, 9.2-inch or 12-inch guns equalled the average obtained in that practice.

	Weight of projectile (pounds) hitting an enemy in 10 minutes.	Relative value.
Two 6-inch guns	840	1
Two 9.2-inch guns	2,812	3.3
Two 12-inch guns	4,250	5

The great superiority of the 12-inch gun is shown at this range, which was a little under 6,000 yards; and is less than the probable mean battle range, the figures are proportionately in favour of the lighter gun.

2. *The increase in speed*. – It is admitted that strategically speed is of very great importance. It enables the fleet or fleets possessing it to concentrate at any desired spot as quickly as possible, and it must therefore exercise an important influence on the course of a naval war, rapid concentration being one of the chief factors of success.

But it is often contended that tactically speed is of little value, although it gives the choice range and enables the disposition, or line of bearing, of a fleet to be rapidly changed. The fact is often overlooked that high speed is a necessity now that long range hitting is possible, for the greater the distance between the opposing line in a fleet action the greater the space to be traversed in order to *gain* or *maintain* a commanding position with respect to the enemy's line.

3. *Size and Cost*. – In both these respects the 'Dreadnought' compares favourably with the battleships projected by the foreign Powers, and it may be stated that of the four next naval powers to Britain, two propose building ships of equal size and cost, and two of greater size and greater cost.

The 'Invincibles' are larger and more costly than other armoured cruisers to be built by foreign Powers, but the speed of the latter is inferior to that of many of the cruisers already afloat, and such vessels would be little use attached to a fleet of 'Dreadnoughts,' whereas the three 'Invincibles,' with their fine speed and great gun power, will ensure an unwilling enemy being brought to action, or should the enemy be anxious to fight, they will be able to select the most advantageous position from which to attack the enemy and support the Battle Fleet.

LEFT This particularly impressive view of *Dreadnought* shows features such as the configuration of boats on the boat deck plus the torpedo-net booms lying flush against the hull. (NMRN)

AN IDEAL BRITISH STANDARD BATTLESHIP.
(AS SHE WOULD APPEAR AT SEA.)

[Frontispiece.

Displacement, 17,000 tons.   Guns: Twelve 12-inch.   Armour: 12".   Speed, 24 kts.   *See the Article in PART III.*

LEFT A book plate from *c*1906 presents a vision of the ideal British battleship, although if the forward guns were fired, life on the low bridge would be particularly uncomfortable on this particular ship. *(NMRN)*

The defence presented in this passage is robust, and other parts of the document lay out in meticulous detail the thinking and data behind the warship type. Whatever the detractors might say, however, there was little denying the fact that the rest of the world quickly bought into the idea of the dreadnought type.

The effect

Once *Dreadnought* was released to the world's view, there was also a curiously positive type of problem from the British. For *Dreadnought* posed a strategic threat. In 1906, the Royal Navy had an undoubted numerical superiority in warships, and one that could be maintained by British shipbuilding capacity. By launching a new type of ship that rendered all previous battleship designs obsolete, Britain was intentionally creating a level playing field in which, given the industrial might emerging in countries such as Germany and the United States, it might lose dominance.

It was a concern that regularly emerged in Parliament in one form or another. One can sense such a concern in this debate quoted

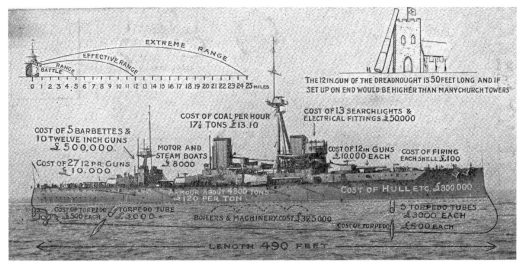

LEFT Once *Dreadnought* was no longer secret, the Admiralty was keen to convey the industrial and military power embodied in the ship, as this contemporary picture demonstrates. *(NMRN)*

in *Hansard* from August 1909, between Birmingham North MP John Middlemore and the Financial Secretary to the Treasury, Reginald McKenna:

Mr. MIDDLEMORE asked how many British battleships included in the Dilke Return of Fleets, dated 31st March 1904, have been removed from the effective list; and how many battleships not included in that Return have since been laid down or provided for?

Mr. McKENNA The number of British battleships included in the Dilke Return of Fleets, dated 31st March 1904, which have been removed from the effective list, is 12. The number of battleships not included in that Return which have since been laid down or provided for, is 15.

HC Deb 04 August 1909, vol. 8, *c*1836

The Admiralty, and eventually the British public, therefore swung squarely behind the dreadnought building programme, pumping millions of pounds and man hours into outstripping the rivals, especially once a startled Germany entered the naval arms race in earnest with the laying down of its *Nassau* class of dreadnoughts (consisting of *Nassau*, *Westfalen*, *Rheinland* and *Posen*) in June to August 1907.

It was an arms race that Britain won, or at least did so by the outbreak of the First World War. Official British tables of ship production published around 1910 proudly declared

that the average contract production time for a dreadnought battleship was 24 months, as opposed to the 36 months it took for Germany to produce a similar vessel. So it was that between 1906 and 1914, Britain manufactured and commissioned no fewer than 29 dreadnought or super dreadnoughts (the latter is explained below), against the output of 17 vessels by the Germans. By 1920, which is effectively when the dreadnought type ceased to be made in Britain, a total of 35 of these great vessels had graced the waves. Naval historian Angus Konstam points out that this Herculean shipbuilding effort cost the British nation a total of £151 million.

Nor were the dreadnoughts the only focus of the British naval output during these epic years. Running adjacent to the battleship building was also the development of the new 'battlecruiser' type. The battlecruiser was also conceived, from 1904, as an 'all-big-gun' warship so that it could trade shells at long range with the biggest enemy vessels. Yet unlike the dreadnoughts, the battlecruisers were to have less-substantial armour, the trade-off being the speed required to deploy quickly and decisively to trouble spots as they flared up. Thus, while the *Dreadnought* had 11in belt armour and a speed of 21 knots, the *Invincible* – the lead ship of the *Invincible* class of battlecruisers (*Invincible*, *Indomitable*, *Inflexible*) – had just 6in of belt armour but a top speed of more than 25 knots, even while carrying a main armament

BELOW *Dreadnought* seen just after her launch on 10 February 1906. The ship suffered some hull damage, which was soon repaired, following a basin trial accident on 3 December. *(NMRN)*

RIGHT *Dreadnought* drops her starboard anchor. The anchor type was the Wasteney-Smith stockless anchor, with flukes limited to 45° movement. *(NMRN)*

of 10 ×12in guns. Fisher became highly invested in the battlecruiser type, even seeing it as superior to the dreadnoughts. Indeed, the large battlecruisers that emerged over the next 20 years often had little to distinguish them from the dreadnoughts in power and dimensions. Thus to the pre-war British output of 29 dreadnoughts, we should also add 9 battlecruisers, although in this field the margin of superiority compared to the Germans was slimmer – Tirpitz's navy launched seven battlecruisers during the same period.

Although this book concentrates squarely on dreadnoughts and super dreadnoughts, we must also recognise that the battlecruiser also stirred the passions of the world's admiralties. This is illustrated by the following article, published in the *Daily Telegraph* on 15 October 1906; it is insightful because it illustrates how another foreign power, in this case the United States, appeared rather cowed by British naval muscle:

BELOW With some fanfare, and in the presence of other Royal Navy warships, *Dreadnought* is towed out by steam tugs after her launch. *(NMRN)*

New Dreadnoughts – American Opinion
(From our own correspondent)

The important announcement published in the 'Daily Telegraph' yesterday with regard to the construction of such formidable additions to the British Navy as are represented by the 'Inflexible,' 'Indomitable,' and the 'Invincible,' was cabled to America and reproduced textually by every leading paper in America. Today that announcement is the topic of almost universal comment. So far as I can gather from conversations with American experts, the British Admiralty have gained another notable victory in ship construction, which will ensure the respect of the entire world, and, more particularly, of those Admiralties 'which naturally wait upon England for the last word in the development of naval service.'

It seems to be admitted, providing your information be confirmed, that Great Britain has attained a consolidation of naval war types which many believed to be impossible. If all the comment I have heard on this side, based admittedly on your exclusive announcement of the details, be true, the British Admiralty, to their great credit, have produced cruisers which easily surpass most of the battleships afloat, including the American.

'The contention,' to quote one American authority, 'so often advanced, that the ideal ship must sooner or later combine harmoniously the variant essentials of the two supreme types of the fighting line, the gun energy and protection of the battleship, with the mobility of the cruiser, has for excellent reasons been no less promptly denied. This has been based upon the assumption that the functions of each were, after a certain point, obviously dissimilar. The attempt to concentrate in one construction so many diverse energies is therefore a matter of the highest importance to warship designers.

Daily Telegraph, 15 October 1906

The fact that 'every leading newspaper in America' showed interest in the emergence of the battlecruiser suggests the impact that naval matters carried at this time was easily equivalent to the media stare on nuclear proliferation during the 1960s–80s. The reference to 'another notable victory' suggests, even allowing for some flattery, that the dreadnoughts and the battlecruisers were internationally regarded as the new standard of warship design, to which others must aspire and seek to build. The fact that Germany almost immediately switched its focus to dreadnought-type battleships and battlecruisers was clear proof of that, from a country less deferential towards Britain than the United States at that time.

So there is little doubt that on the world stage the dreadnought was a true game-changer, a warship that affected the very strategic composition of the global powers. Yet before we go on to analyse the evolution of the British dreadnought type, we should stop again and consider the classic claim that the dreadnought rendered all other warships obsolete. A useful lens through which to view this debate is a

BELOW *Dreadnought* viewed from the port rear. Note how 'hidden' the 12in 'X' turret is between the aft funnel and the mainmast. *(NMRN))*

British newspaper report from *The Times*, published on 18 July 1910, and squarely titled 'What is a Dreadnought?' Given that the public was now aware of just how much of their economy was being poured into these hulking vessels, the newspaper obviously felt that some technical clarification was needed. The article also provides a useful window on what other nations were doing at the same time:

If we look in another direction, it might perhaps at first sight appear as if the distinctive feature of a Dreadnought consisted in her being equipped with an armament of what in American phraseology is termed the 'all-big-gun single-calibre' type. That was no doubt the true differentia of the original Dreadnought, which is armed for the purposes of a fleet action with ten 12-inch guns and no others, her remaining armament of 24 twelve-pounder guns being intended only for defence against torpedo attack. It is also the true differentia of the later British Dreadnoughts, though in their case the anti-torpedo armament is of larger calibre. But it is not the true differentia of many of the more recent so-called Dreadnoughts built or building for foreign Navies. The French Danton class is to carry four 12-inch and twelve 9.4-inch guns, thus approximating very closely to our own Lord Nelson type, which is armed with four 12-inch and ten 9.2-inch guns, together in each case with a powerful anti-torpedo armament. The German Nassau type carries twelve 11-inch and twelve 5.9-inch guns, together with an additional anti-torpedo armament. The armament of the projected Italian Dreadnoughts is not given in the Dilke Return [an annual statement of serviceable warships, named after its moving force, Sir Charles Dilke] and though some details are furnished in the 'Naval Annual,' they are there stated to be uncertain. In the United States the Delaware type now completed is armed with ten 12-inch and fourteen 5-inch guns, together with an anti-torpedo armament, though it may be that the 5-inch armament is intended mainly for defence against torpedo attack. The Florida and Arkansas types now building are similarly but more powerfully armed. The Japanese ships of the Kawachi

type are to carry twelve 12-inch, ten 6-inch, and fourteen 4.7-inch guns, the latter no doubt for defence against torpedo attack. Russia alone of the Powers enumerated in the Dilke Return appears to approximate in the ships of the Sevastopol type to the original Dreadnought differentia, since these ships are to be armed with twelve 12-inch and twelve 4.7-inch guns, together with an additional anti-torpedo armament of a lighter character. It is clear, then, from this enumeration that the 'all-big-gun single-calibre' armament is not a true and distinctive differentia of many of the so-called Dreadnoughts now built and building by the leading naval Powers of the world. Such an armament is to be found in some of them, but not in all, and apparently not in the majority. …

ABOVE HMS *Indefatigable* was a Royal Navy battlecruiser launched in 1909 and commissioned in 1911. Battlecruisers were the important counterpoint to dreadnought design around this period.

BELOW The French continued to launch pre-dreadnought designs even after the launch of *Dreadnought*. The *Danton* class, seen here in plan, was equipped with four steam turbines like *Dreadnought*, but had a mixed armament of 12in, 9.5in and 3in guns.

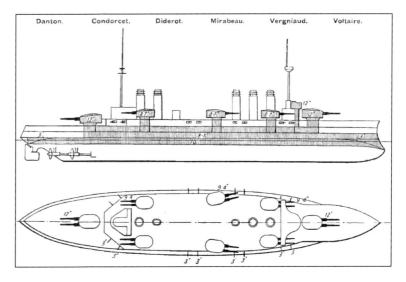

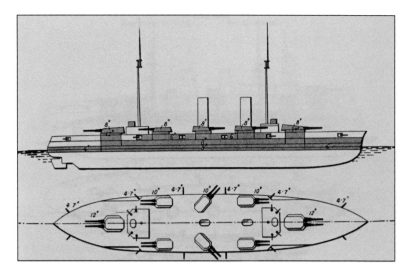

In other words, when we speak of a Dreadnought nowadays we mean nothing more than a warship of the first class which has been designed and constructed at some time posterior to the year 1906. All such ships are no doubt somewhat faster, in many cases much faster, much more heavily armed, and of larger displacement, in many cases of much larger displacement, than the 'capital ships' still fit to lie in a line which immediately preceded them; but development in these several directions is only in the natural order of evolution – an order of evolution which has been more or less continuous ever since the first ironclad was constructed – and does not itself constitute a differentia which separates the original Dreadnought and all 'capital

ships' since constructed from all those which preceded her. It may thus very well be held that the growing habit of talking about Dreadnoughts only, and thinking in Dreadnoughts only, is not unlikely to lead to much confusion in the public mind, and even to some confusion in naval policy.

This is a subtle and sophisticated argument. The writer explains how the dreadnoughts are, in real material terms, evolutions of the battleship design, not an actual revolution. Furthermore, he also exposes how the all-big-gun concept was not watertight, especially when looking at developments further afield, where the secondary armament remained robust. Indeed, if we look closely at the continual development of the British dreadnought, we do detect a shifting movement in philosophy from 1906 onwards.

From dreadnought to super dreadnoughts

As noted above, having levelled the playing field with the launch of *Dreadnought*, the priority for the Admiralty was then to maintain the momentum of the initial lead with a continuous, high-tempo shipbuilding programme. This it did immediately with the development of the *Bellerophon* class of dreadnoughts, three vessels (*Bellerophon*, *Superb* and *Temeraire*) that were largely

identical models of the benchmark ship, with some key differences. (The essential evolutionary differences between each of the major classes of dreadnought and super dreadnought will be explored in Chapter 2.) The first of these ships was laid down on 3 December 1906 and the last of them was completed, ready for service, in May 1909. But this was just the beginning. Between 1907 and 1914, two more classes of dreadnought were completed – the *St Vincent* class (*Collingwood*, *St Vincent* and *Vanguard*), the *Colossus* class (*Colossus* and *Hercules*), plus two independent battleships of the series (*Neptune* and *Agincourt*). Although the timescale of production was particularly rapid, the dreadnought warships nevertheless underwent a significant series of changes. The layout of the main armament on deck was radically revised, shifting towards a centreline-only, fore and aft superfiring arrangement of the main guns, rather than having the dual wing and amidships turrets. The secondary battery, the omission of which formed the grounding rationale for the original *Dreadnought*, steadily crept back in, both in response to tactical considerations and also through acknowledging the developments in rival foreign dreadnought vessels. Superstructure arrangements changed accordingly, and also in the attempt to provide a better observation platform for the gunnery spotting top, up high on the foremast.

Such adjustments helped keep the British dreadnoughts in the line of battle, but once the arms race was under way, speed of production was far from the only consideration that came into play. Any arms race forms the ideal conditions for technological advancement, and the pre-1914 naval competition was no exception. For towards the end of the first decade of the 20th century, the British Admiralty began to receive intelligence about the gunnery formats of rival dreadnought designs. More specifically, there was evidence that the American, Japanese and, most worryingly, German navies were looking into the possibility of mounting main guns of a calibre larger than 12in – specifically 13.5in, 14in and 15in calibres. These offered greater range, more destructive capability, a flatter trajectory, and therefore improved accuracy and fire control.

These were not just scare stories. Over in

the United States, the US Navy launched the USS *New York*, the lead ship of a two-ship class, on 30 October 1912. Once fully fitted out, this warship sported 10 × 14in guns plus a hefty secondary armament of 21 × 5in guns. From 1912 the Japanese also began building battleships with 14in guns, beginning with the *Fuso*-class vessels *Fuso* and *Yamashiro*. Germany actually stuck with the 12in guns for most of the pre-war period, but in 1913–15 laid down both the *Mackensen* class of battlecruiser and the *Bayern* class of super dreadnought,

ABOVE The USS *Alabama* was an *Illinois*-class pre-dreadnought commissioned in 1890. Main armament was four 13in guns, supported by 14 × 6in guns in hull-mounted sponsons. *(LOC)*

BELOW The *Yamashiro*, here seen during the fitting-out process, was one of the new generation of Japanese dreadnoughts. She was a *Fuso*-class battleship, and was sunk, along with her sister ship *Fuso*, in the Philippines campaign in 1944.

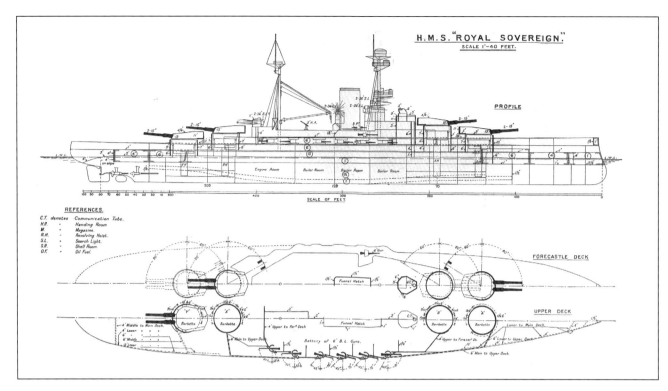

H.M.S. "ROYAL SOVEREIGN."
SCALE 1"—40 FEET.

PROFILE

REFERENCES.
C.T. denotes   Communication Tube.
H.R.   "   Handing Room
M.   "   Magazine.
R.H.   "   Revolving Hoist.
S.L.   "   Search Light.
S.R.   "   Shell Room.
O.F.   "   Oil Fuel.

SCALE OF FEET

FORECASTLE DECK

UPPER DECK

ABOVE A plan of HMS *Royal Sovereign*, **the epitome of the super dreadnought. With 15in main guns, she had the heaviest of the super dreadnought armament configurations.**

BELOW HMS *Iron Duke* **profile as fitted.** *(National Maritime Museum)*

both of which had 8 × 35cm guns. France also began a gravitation towards heavier guns as building began on the Bretagne-class from 1912, each vessel of the class to be equipped with 10 × 34cm (13in) guns.

Picking up on the first rumblings of at least some of these developments around 1909, the British knew that the dreadnought needed an upgrade if it was to face the future threats. The result was the series of ships we label as 'super dreadnoughts', and their production began with the *Orion* class (*Conqueror*, *Monarch*, *Orion* and *Thunderer*) as part of the 1909 shipbuilding

programme. Gone were the days of the wing turrets; these ships each had 10–13.5in Mk V guns all mounted on the centreline, with 'B' (fore) and 'X' (aft) turrets superimposed over the 'A' and 'Y' turrets respectively. The *Orions* were also more substantial vessels than the preceding *Colossus* class of dreadnoughts. They were longer, with a displacement increase of more than 2,000 tons, plus they had some armour increases. The British super dreadnoughts had arrived.

There would be a total of five classes of British super dreadnought – *Orion*, *King*

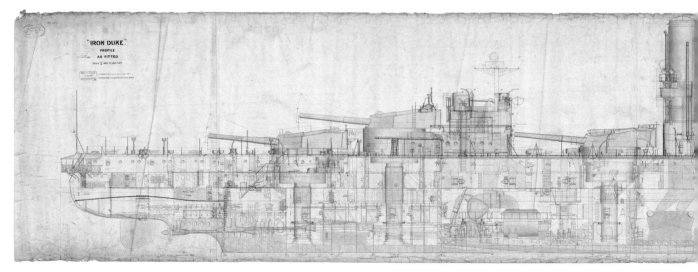

George V, *Iron Duke*, *Queen Elizabeth* and
Royal Sovereign – which together constituted
22 vessels, plus two privately built warships,
HMS *Erin* and HMS *Canada*. The super
dreadnoughts were naked expressions of
force, and with the launch and commissioning
of each new class they grew in power, size
and destructive potential. Again the details of
this development are explored in more detail
in Chapter 2, but it is worth mentioning some
notable landmarks.

In the *Iron Duke* class, launched in 1912–13,
the secondary armament was upped to 6in
guns, replacing the 4in QF guns of previous
dreadnoughts and super dreadnoughts. The
move was rational – the increased threat
of smaller vessels such as destroyers, light
cruisers and fast torpedo boats meant that the
secondary armament now had more of a role
to play – but it essentially signalled the end of
the dreadnought-type vessel as an 'all-big-
gun' design. This move faced little resistance,
not least because Fisher had retired in 1910.
Not that the focus on big guns had dimmed.
With the news about American and Japanese
naval gunnery developments, the Director of
Naval Ordnance (DNO) decided to fit the *Queen
Elizabeth* class with the new 15in Mk I BL
(breech-loading) guns, eight of these monsters
in total. The *Royal Sovereign* class also adopted
this firepower. It cannot have been anything
other than awe-inspiring to witness a broadside
ripping out from one of these great vessels.

The super dreadnoughts were the apotheosis
of a new generation of vessels that had first run

ABOVE The Argentine dreadnought *Rividavia* had an interesting gun layout,
with twin superfiring 12in turrets fore and aft, plus two further 12in turrets
amidships and offset.

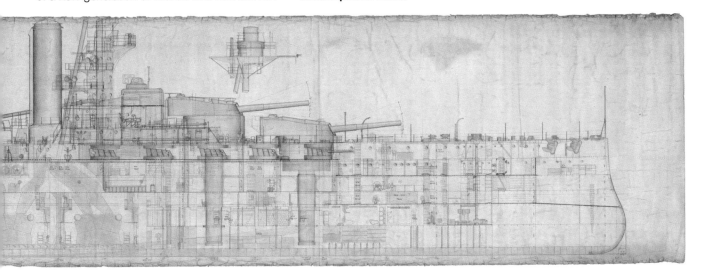

down the slipways in 1906. Since the launch of *Dreadnought*, the battleships of Britain and the other major international naval players had grown immensely in size and power, their massive silhouettes and brooding gunnery suggesting that nothing could challenge their authority. This was not to be the case.

End of an era

It is one of the ironies of the dreadnoughts and super dreadnoughts that for all their brutish destructive capability, they would be so infrequently used in warfare. Of course, the greatest clash of these leviathans came on 31 May–1 June 1916, when the British Grand Fleet exchanged monumental blows with the German High Seas Fleet at the Battle of Jutland. The *Queen Elizabeth*-class *Warspite*, for example, fired no fewer than 259 15in shells during this battle. Yet Jutland is salient because of its singular rarity. In fact, most of the time the great battleships simply manoeuvred warily, offering big-gun protection to other vessels, imposing blockades or hunting lesser warships. Battleships were vast and costly systems, and admiralties became generally wary of anything that might put them in harm's way. A great ship of nearly 1,000 men could be dispatched with little more than a single shell-strike at the right (or wrong, depending on your perspective) location. This lesson was learned in Jutland, but it was still being painfully digested during the Second World War – one need only reflect the

fates of ships such as *Hood*, *Bismarck* and *Graf Spee* to understand this point.

Even before the first shots of the First World War were fired, however, prescient voices were realising that the world of naval warfare was changing. One of these voices was Admiral Sir Percy Scott, an influential Navy commander and expert on matters relating to gunnery. In June 1914, Scott published a controversial letter that undermined the whole rationale of Britain's surface fleet, including its capital vessels. Part of that letter is reproduced here:

The introduction of the vessels that swim under water has, in my opinion, entirely done away with the utility of the ships that swim on the top of the water. The submarine causes to disappear three out of five of the functions, defensive and offensive, of a vessel of war, as no man-of-war will dare to come even within sight of a coast that is adequately protected by submarines. The fourth function of a battleship is to attack an enemy's fleet, but there will be no fleet to attack, as it will not be safe for a fleet to put to sea. If by submarines we close egress from the North Sea and Mediterranean, it is difficult to see how our commerce can be much interfered with. Submarines and aeroplanes have entirely revolutionized naval warfare, no fleet can hide itself from the aeroplane eye, and the submarine can deliver a deadly attack even in broad daylight. Naval officers of the future will therefore live

BELOW The *Dreadnought* began a design evolution that led to ultimate battleships such as the German *Tirpitz*, seen here. *Tirpitz*'s career, however, is testimony to the weakening of the battleship rationale. *(US Navy)*

either above the sea or under it. It will be a Navy of youth, for we shall require nothing but boldness and daring. Not only is the open sea unsafe with a flotilla of submarines … I would undertake to get … into any harbour, and sink or materially damage all the ships in that harbour. What we require is an enormous fleet of submarines, airships, and aeroplanes, and a few fast crossers, provided we can find a place to keep them in safety during wartime. In my opinion, as the motor-vehicle has driven the horse from the road, so has the submarine driven the battleship from the sea.

Percy Scott, letter, 1914

With the benefit of our hindsight, the prophetic quality of this passage is startling. Scott placed aviation and submarines at the vanguard of naval warfare, with even the great surface vessels essentially looking for a place to hide during wartime. We need only look ahead to the shy deployments of the *Tirpitz* in the Second World War to see the accuracy of this prediction. Scott was also writing at a time when he couldn't see the eventual combat force of naval aviation, a time when US dive-bombers and torpedo bombers would reduce the largest battleship ever made, the Japanese *Yamato*, to nothing more than useless, blistered metal.

Hence if we look at the fates of the British dreadnoughts and super dreadnoughts, they tend to be less than glorious. Most were eventually sold for scrap and broken up in the 1920s–40s, the ships looking dated in an era that brought aircraft carriers, U-boats and manoeuvre warfare. For others came violent end, though rarely in open battle against other vessels. HMS *Vanguard* (*St Vincent* class) was accidentally destroyed in a magazine explosion on 9 July 1917. Super dreadnought *Audacious* (*King George V* class) sank after hitting a mine on 27 October 1914. HMS *Barham* (*Queen Elizabeth* class) survived one world war only to be destroyed in another – it was torpedoed in the Mediterranean on 25 November 1941, the after magazine exploding as it capsized, ripping the ship apart and contributing to a final death toll of 841 men. By the time this occurred, the British had already witnessed the tragic power of submarine warfare against capital vessels,

when HMS *Royal Oak* (*Royal Sovereign*-class) was sunk on 14 October 1939 in the supposedly safe waters of Scapa Flow by *U-47*.

Britain, and other nations, continued to produce battleships after the super dreadnoughts, but by the end of the Second World War the battleship as a type was in its twilight years. That said, while the tactical performance of the dreadnoughts and super dreadnoughts is open to question, their influence over world politics, and over the lives of the thousands of men who built or crewed them, is undeniable.

ABOVE The threat. ***U-534***, a German Type IXC/40 U-boat, stands at Birkenhead Docks. Submarines undercut the power proposition offered by battleships, as demonstrated in events such as the sinking of *Royal Oak* in 1939. *(Paul Adams)*

BELOW HMS *Vanguard*, a *St Vincent*-class dreadnought launched in 1909, was destroyed in an accidental magazine explosion on 9 July 1917.

Chapter Two

The layout of the ship

The dreadnoughts were living communities afloat. The layout of each ship had to facilitate not only violent naval combat, but also the daily processes that enabled the ship to perform countless more mundane duties at home and abroad.

OPPOSITE *Dreadnought*'s protective deck under construction, looking at the aft of the ship. Rivet holes have been drilled in the hull plates, each rivet typically 4–5 diameters from the next. *(NMRN)*

To get a sense of how dreadnoughts and super dreadnoughts were structurally organised in general, we need to go back to the grandfather of them all – the original *Dreadnought*. By describing how this seminal ship was designed, we are better placed to understand the thinking behind the many subsequent changes and design upgrades implemented between 1906 and the early 1920s.

General construction features

Some basic data about the *Dreadnought* gives us context. The overall length of the warship was 526ft, the length between perpendiculars was 490ft and the ship's beam was 82ft. With a normal load, the battleship's displacement was 17,110 tons, but at maximum load that figure rose to 21,845 tons. At normal load the draught was 28ft, rising to 29ft for deep loading.

Dreadnought was intended for high performance, and its hull structure reflected that priority. Looking at the ship in transverse profile, we see that it had a very square profile amidships, with a flat bottom and near vertical sides, much like that found on the earlier *Lord Nelson* class of pre-dreadnought vessel. This type of hull form was good for enabling the ship to handle its displacement with a stable sea performance, reducing the level of roll. However, flat-bottomed boats have an increased drag, the compensation for which came in the design of *Dreadnought*'s stern and bow. At the bow, particular attention was paid to the design of the stem (the underwater projection from the bow). The stem derived from the ram fitted to an earlier generation of ships, but by 1906 ramming was a rare tactic indeed, except when used against much lighter, smaller and more fragile vessels. However, the stem had the ancillary benefit of reducing the bow wave, and therefore reducing drag, thus *Dreadnought* was fitted with a smoothly curved profile. To improve the ship's manoeuvrability, and to provide space for the propellers and rudder, the stern featured a long cut-up.

Another characteristic of *Dreadnought*'s hull design was its double bottom. This not only gave the ship greater survivability in case of underwater damage, it also provided a cellular space for the bulk storage of oil. The issue of survivability in the age of big-gun and torpedo warfare was naturally uppermost in the minds of Watts and others as the ship was designed. Beneath the main deck, the ship was divided by a network of longitudinal and transverse bulkheads, these featuring 8in armour to the aft bulkhead, protecting vital features such as the shell rooms and magazines. Watertight doors in many of the bulkheads could be swung shut to contain flooding.

The issue of armoured protection was a complicated one back in 1906, and in some areas of military development remains so to this day. The essential problem is that the

more armour is applied, the heavier and slower the ship. So, any ship design was essentially a trade-off between speed (in itself a key ingredient of protection) and armoured protection. The distribution of *Dreadnought*'s armour by weight was as follows:

- Side armour – 1,940 tons
- Decks, gratings – 1,350 tons
- Magazines – 250 tons
- Steering-gear compartment – 100 tons
- Barbettes – 1,260 tons
- Bridge – 100 tons.

These figures are interesting, especially when held in comparison with the pre-dreadnought *Lord Nelson* class of warships. Only in deck/grating and barbette armour do the weight figures exceed those of *Lord Nelson*, despite the fact that *Lord Nelson* was a smaller and lighter ship, which might lead us to conclude that *Dreadnought* was in fact under-armoured. The picture defies a simplistic conclusion, however. In terms of the side protection, *Dreadnought* had some vulnerabilities. The side armour consisted of an 11in main belt, shielding the ship's machinery from torpedo attack or a low shell-strike, with 8in armour over the rest of the ship's sides. However, depending on the loading and therefore displacement of the ship, the main belt generally sat either on or below the waterline, leaving the vessel above the waterline with limited protection, especially from plunging

fire. John Roberts, in his recommended work *The Battleship Dreadnought*, notes that:

> A better arrangement would have resulted from a uniform belt thickness, although the maximum that could have been provided without increasing the displacement would have been 9.5in. Alternatively, the belt could have been raised to a higher level, but this would have altered the stability and may well have involved an undesirable increase in beam. It does not seem that the armour arrangement was seen at the time as particularly inadequate, as the same basic arrangement was followed in all the later British 12-in gun battleships, although a number of

ABOVE In this view of the *Dreadnought* we can see one of the bulkhead sections at the front with an access passage in the middle. *(NMRN)*

BELOW A fine view of *Dreadnought*'s fore end under construction, clearly showing the ram-like prow. *(NMRN)*

BELOW *Dreadnought*'s stern section. Just below the wooden gangway, at the very rear of the ship, would be the opening of the stern torpedo tube. *(NMRN)*

- Barbettes – 11/8/4in
- Turrets – 11in sides/13in back/3in roof
- Conning tower – 11in sides/4in floor/ 3in roof
- Signal tower – 8in sides/4in floor/3in roof
- Main deck – 0.75in
- Middle deck – 3–1.75in (thickest armour over 'A' and 'Y' magazines)
- Lower deck – 4–1.5in (4in armour around 'A' and 'Y' barbettes/3in armour over steering gear).

We can note from these figures that *Dreadnought* was indeed most vulnerable to enemy plunging fire, given that its deck armour was the lightest of all its armour plate. Again, it would take the hard lessons of combat to educate the Admiralty about the need for more resilient deck armour.

Superstructure

Looking broadly at the externals of *Dreadnought*, the first major feature that we encounter working back down the ship from the bow (having passed the three hawse pipes for the anchor chain plus ground tackle, and two 12in guns on the starboard side) is the 'A' turret, housing twin 12in guns. This turret was one of five on *Dreadnought;* there were a further two set on the beams – 'P' barbette on the port and 'Q' barbette on the starboard – and two rearward-facing barbettes on the centreline consisting of 'X' barbette just behind the aft funnel and 'Y' barbette overlooking the stern (aft deck). The 24 12-pdr guns were dotted around the forecastle deck and upper deck.

Returning to the front of the ship, directly behind 'A' barbette was the elevated bridge and conning tower, and key command spaces such as the navigating platform, chart house and compass platform. Viewed from any distance, the other most salient features of the ship were the two masts. The foremast, set a short (and ultimately problematic) distance behind the forward funnel, was a tripod structure, with internal ladders within each strut to enable ascent to the searchlight platform and the rangefinder-equipped foretop. The shorter mainmast was located to the rear of the aft funnel, and featured searchlight mountings and an elevated main top.

detail improvements were made, including increasing the depth of the main belt.

John Roberts,
The Battleship Dreadnought

Roberts goes on to point out, however, that lengthwise the 11in side armour also stopped short of giving full protection to both 'A' turret and 'Y' barbette, a fact that left the ship exposed at critical points. (Belt armour protection forward was 6in, while aft it was just 4in.) Only the salutary experience provided by the Battle of Jutland in 1916 provided the impetus to strengthen these exposed points.

In terms of the armour attached to other parts of the ship, the following depths applied:

Between these two poles another structure worth noting, located on the boat deck, was the signal tower, atop which was fitted another 9ft Barr and Stroud rangefinder.

On the boat deck, somewhere obviously had to be found for the small craft. Here was something of a problem for the designers. Generally speaking, the *Dreadnought* was a rather claustrophobic design, by virtue of the locations of 'P' and 'Q' barbettes, which squeezed the superstructure inwards at the middle. There was also the blast to be considered. If these guns were fired, especially along a line that ranged close to parallel with the ship's sides, blast damage would occur to surrounding structures, hence the superstructure around the gun muzzles had to be pared back to the minimum. The boats also had to be placed intelligently to avoid blast damage. There were eight boats in total clustered around the deck on derrick mounts. To the front of the deck there were two 32ft cutters (one either side), and a further 32ft cutter or 27ft whaler set just behind the foremast. Around the rear funnel and signal tower six further boats – (1) a 16ft dinghy; (2) 27ft whaler; (3) 45ft steam pinnace; (4) 40ft

BELOW *Dreadnought* is seen here in the process of coaling, a filthy business that would often require ship cleaning afterwards, especially if manual hoists were used. *(NMRN)*

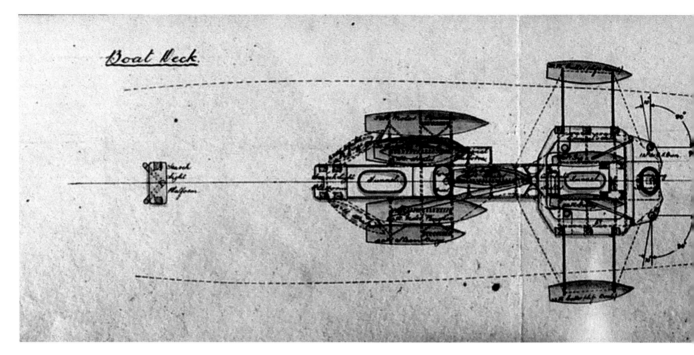

steam barge (for the Admiral's personal use); (5) 13ft 6in balsa raft; and (6) either a 42ft launch, 36ft pinnace or 27ft whaler.

The rear forecastle and upper decks of the ship were largely given over to the big guns of 'X' and 'Y' turrets, twin 12in guns mounted in each turret. This part of the ship also had a liberal sprinkling of 12-pdr guns including, originally, two atop each of the main gun turrets plus three set further back on the upper deck,

as guardians over the stern. The guns set on the turrets were eventually removed, it being discovered that the blast of the main guns in action was detrimental to both the 12-pdr guns and to their crews.

Below decks

Dreadnought was divided into seven deck levels:

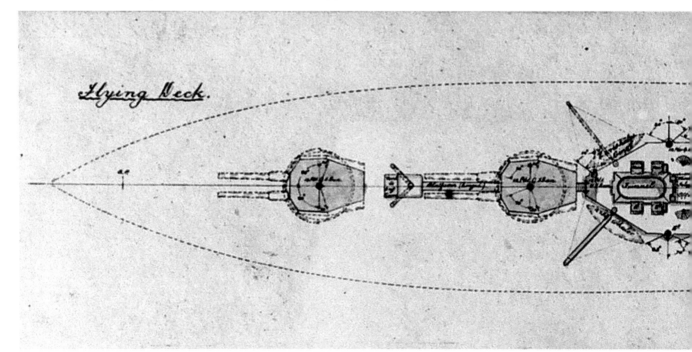

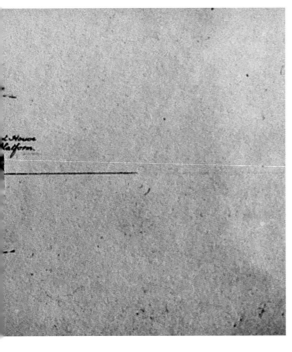

- ■ Flying (forecastle) deck
- ■ Upper deck
- ■ Main deck
- ■ Middle deck
- ■ Lower deck
- ■ Platform deck
- ■ Hold.

Across these decks, the ship's complement brought the vessel to life, from the gunners manning the main guns on the upper deck, to the stokers down in the hold, plying their grimy trade. A full explanation of every room, compartment and function within these decks is impossible here, so some broad brushstrokes are necessary. One general point should be noted early on. Typically, Royal Navy battleships featured officers' accommodation towards the rear of the ship, where it was better shielded from the noise of the engines and experienced reduced movement at sea compared to the front of the ship. In *Dreadnought*'s case, the officers were berthed forward on the upper deck, keeping the officers close to the command centres of the ship, despite the fact that this gave them smaller accommodation and a more intimate acquaintance with the throb and hum of key pieces of ship's machinery, such as the diesel dynamos, refrigeration plant and hydraulic pumping engines. Nevertheless, the arrangement caused some raised eyebrows among the wider naval community.

The officers' accommodation ranged from the luxury of the Admiral's sleeping cabin – plus associated dining cabin, saloon and his very own bathroom – down to the cabins for junior officers, principally clustered along the port and starboard upper deck amidships, plus an internal grouping between the flanking gun barbettes. The exigencies of accommodation, however, could

BELOW

Dreadnought's flying (forecastle) deck, the plan showing both the position of the main armament, plus the range of traverse for the forward 12in turret. (NMRN)

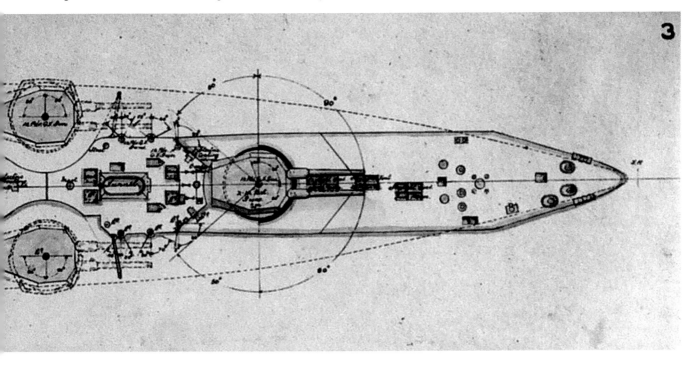

3

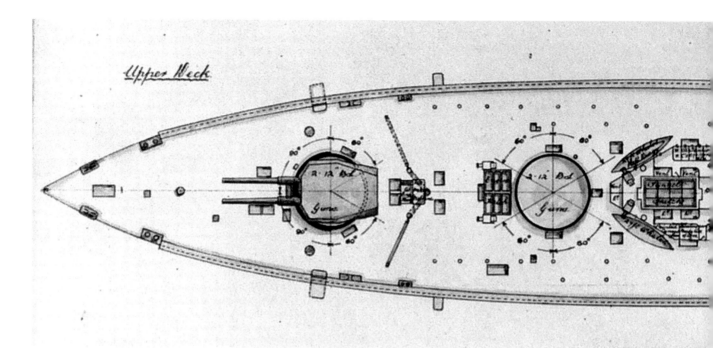

ABOVE *Dreadnought's* upper deck plan. The front of the deck is dominated by officers' spaces, including cabins for the Admiral's stewards and cooks. *(NMRN)*

mean that the junior officer might find himself consigned to all manner of nooks and crannies. The typical officer's cabin consisted of a bunk with under-bed storage unit, a washstand and bottle rack, a small bookshelf plus a desk and chair. While this was certainly a step up from the rather improvised feel of the accommodation of other ranks, with hammocks slung from a variety of locations, most officers were by no means what we would describe as 'comfortable', as the memoirs of one Lieutenant Lionel Dawson explain:

The mess-decks were small and cramped, and, being aft, most inconvenient for the internal economy of the ship. She was the first battleship in which the greater part of the officers' quarters were forward. It was by no means an unqualified advantage. Cabins were small and distributed all over the ship, wherever room could be found for them. My first cabin was in one of the mess-decks aft, and a horrible place it was to live in. From it one had to walk half the length of the ship

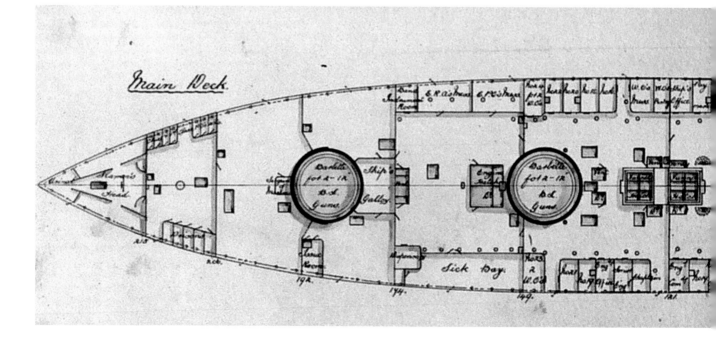

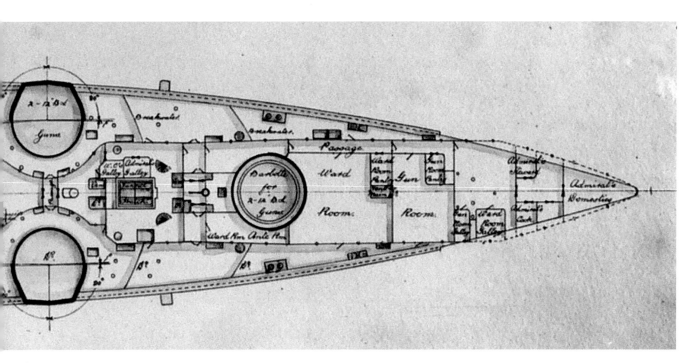

to the officers' bathroom. My second was forward, all mixed up with the chain cables and a Diesel engine that provided an auxiliary supply light for the fore part of the ship when necessary, and whose vibrations made life in its vicinity very uncomfortable when it was running. There was a good wardroom forward – very light and airy, and on the upper deck; the Admiral's quarters, on the deck below, were also good.

Dawson, *Flotillas: A Hard-Lying Story*

Dawson's views throw additional controversy on to the issue of the location of the officers' quarters, giving the impression of a rather fragmented order. Other key rooms on the upper and main decks were the prisons, sick bay and dispensary, engineer's office, chaplain's cabin and paymaster's cabin and band instrument room.

As we start to descend deeper into the ship, we find a steady transition in purpose from accommodation to victualling, engineering

BELOW Working down lower into *Dreadnought*, the plan here is of the main deck. Along the sides of this deck we find most of the senior officers' accommodation. *(NMRN)*

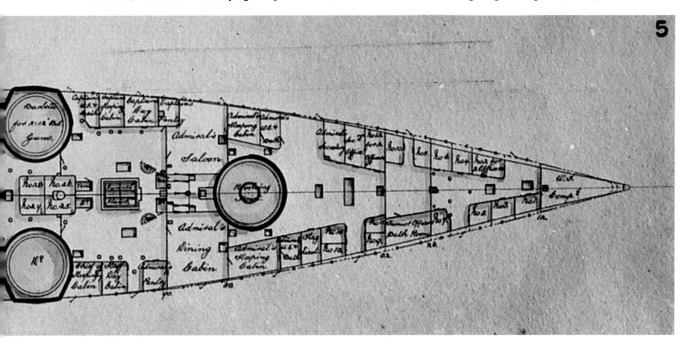

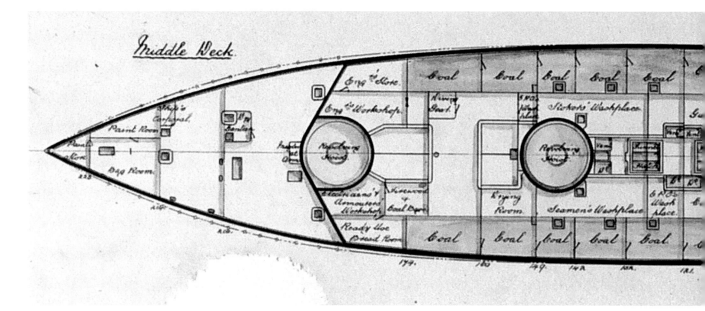

THE SHIP'S COMPLEMENT

Dreadnought's complement changed significantly over its lifetime, ranging from fewer than 700 in 1907 to more than 800 by the end of the First World War. At the time of its Experimental Cruise in 1907, it had a complement of 692 men, 69 of whom were a unit of Royal Marines. Three years later, in January 1910, the manpower had grown to 733 (70 Marines), then 798 (83 Marines) by the following April. Peak manpower came in September 1918, with 830 personnel in total. Of the total crew, around 38% were seamen, 5% boys, 6% officers and 12% Marines. Yet a full 28% were engineering personnel, giving an idea of the technological feat required to keep the ship working and operational.

and weaponry. Although the middle deck contained some accommodation aft, including the petty officers' mess, there was a definite emphasis on more practical spaces. There were numerous stores – for paint, engineering equipment, mechanical spares, food (this deck and the lower deck contained refrigeration machinery), cables, diving gear and gunnery tools – plus engineers' and armourers' workshops (as well as many associated washrooms). Just forward and starboard of 'A' barbette was the chart and chronometer room, and next door aft was the torpedo lobby. There was also equipment and hoists to support the functioning of the 12-pdr guns. Coal bunkers

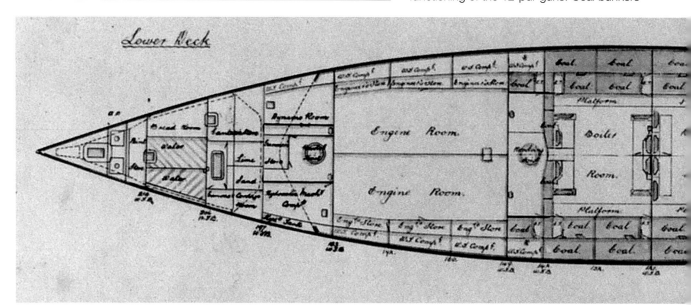

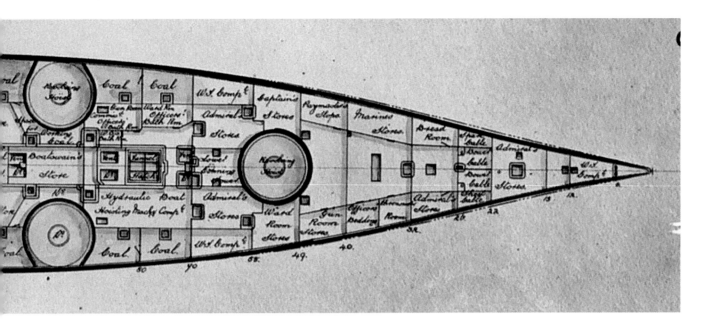

were distributed across much of the port and starboard sides.

Moving down to the lower deck and the platform deck, now the focus of the ship shifted distinctly to its powerplant and to its warfighting role. Dominating these decks were three massive spaces – two boiler rooms and then, in the rear half of the ship, the engine room, with the dynamo space set above the boiler rooms. As these decks were now below the waterline, they were also used extensively for ammunition storage and handling. On the upper deck were working spaces for both 12in and 12-pdr ammunition, and associated hoists, plus a torpedo lobby. On the platform deck were the four torpedo tubes (two aft, two forward) and their torpedo rooms (there was another torpedo tube in the stern), plus the 12in and 12-pdr magazines and, set in four locations along the length of the ship, airtight cases for storing bagged cordite charges. There was also a small-arms magazine.

Finally we get to the bottom of the ship, into the hull. Here were the lowermost sections of the boiler room and the engine room, and from the

ABOVE The middle deck, which was more utilitarian in purpose than the decks above. Note the extent of space required for coal. *(NMRN)*

BELOW Once we reach *Dreadnought*'s lower deck, seen here, engine rooms and boiler spaces dominate. On this deck we also find the working spaces for the 12in ammunition. *(NMRN)*

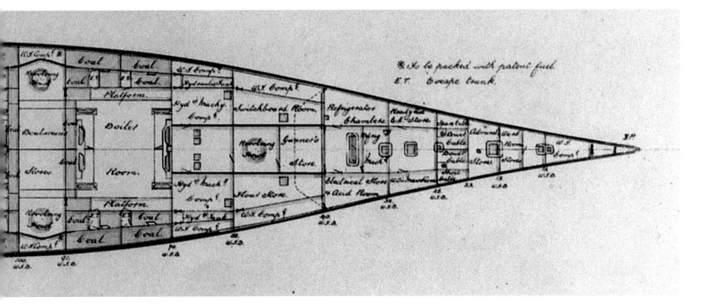

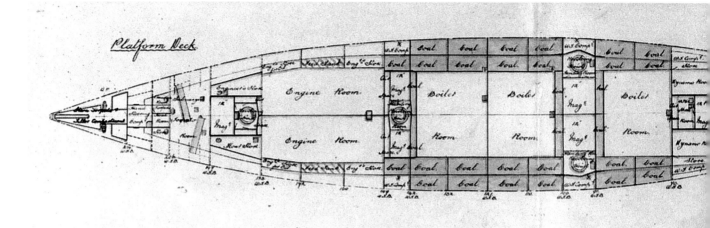

Platform Deck

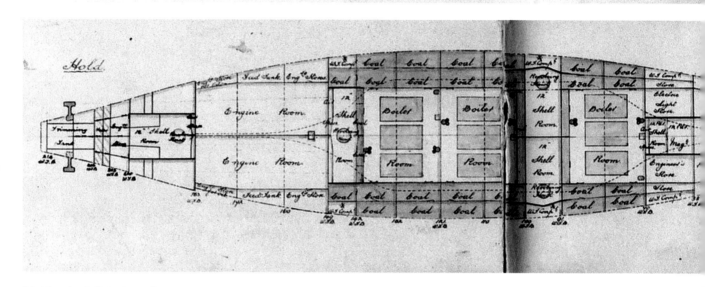

Hold

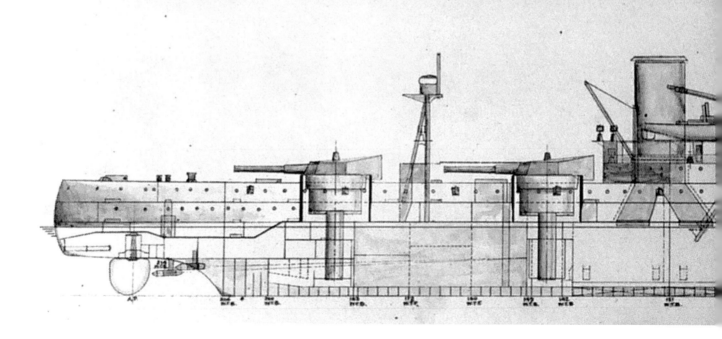

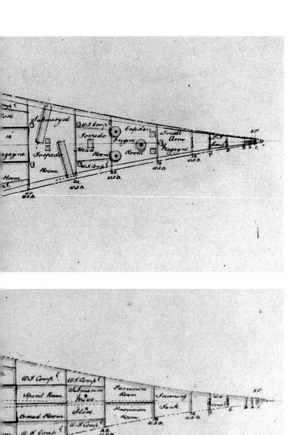

LEFT *Dreadnought*'s platform deck plan also shows the position and angling of the four torpedo tubes, two aft and two forward. Magazines for both the 12in and 12-pdr guns are at this level. *(NMRN)*

latter ran the four housings that held the propeller shafts. Again, there was ammunition storage and handling facilities – a lower magazine for both the 12-pdr and 12in guns, shell rooms for the individual turrets and there was even a store for anti-submarine mines. But the hold was also used for the storage of perishable items – olive oil, flour, bread and other provisions.

We have taken an overview tour of *Dreadnought* as she appeared in 1907. Naturally, this was just the beginning of her service life, and ahead of her was a seemingly endless series of modifications, refits and adjustments to keep her relevant and fighting fit. Rather than chart all these modifications in turn, however, it is more historically useful to look at how the dreadnoughts and super dreadnoughts began to evolve as a type.

LEFT The hold. Note the positioning of the shell rooms – the ammunition hoist trunking ran directly up from here to feed the turrets above. *(NMRN)*

BELOW This profile image of *Dreadnought* illustrates how the main gun turret ammunition machinery descended almost the full depth of the hull. Note the waterline level, placing shell rooms and magazines below water. *(NMRN)*

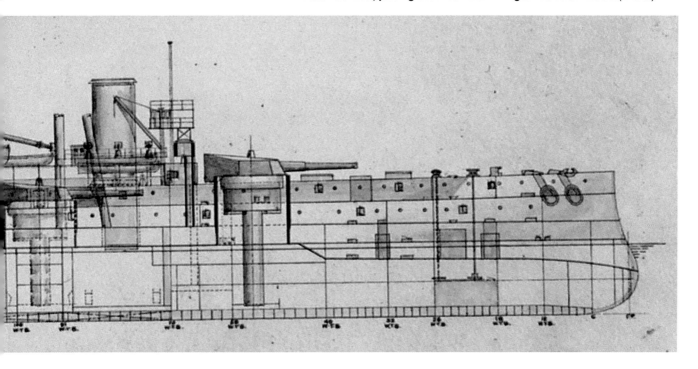

From *Bellerophon* to *Vanguard*

As noted above, the Admiralty realised that if Britain was to maintain its strategic lead internationally, it had to produce the dreadnoughts rapidly. For this reason, the first class of dreadnoughts to appear – the *Bellerophon* class – was little modified from the progenitor warship. There were some incremental changes, however. A problem of the *Dreadnought* was that the smoke from the forward funnel often rose and swirled around the foremast, obscuring the all-important view of those in the foretop position, with their responsibilities for rangefinding and gunnery

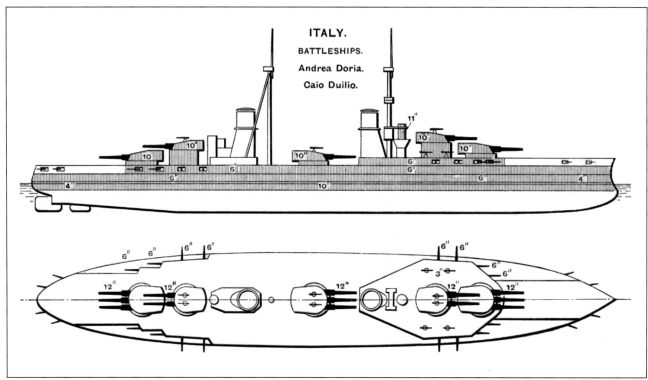

ITALY.

BATTLESHIPS.

Andrea Doria.

Caio Duilio.

control. The *Bellerophon* class attempted to remedy this problem by shifting the tripod foremast in front of the funnel, rather than behind as in the *Dreadnought*, but the problem of smoke remained persistent. There were other changes. The slightly different design meant that the class's armour was somewhat thinner than *Dreadnought*'s, attaining a maximum of 10in around the belt. By way of protective compensation, the *Bellerophon* vessels had watertight bulkheads running the entire length of the ship; on the *Dreadnought* only the magazines were given flood protection. But most interesting was the addition of a significant secondary armament, in the form of 16 × 4in QF guns, although this number was reduced with the eventual removal of the guns that were super-mounted atop the 12in gun turrets – an impractical location if ever there was one.

Three *Bellerophon* warships were laid down and built in 1906–7: *Bellerophon*, *Superb* and *Temeraire*. They were quickly followed by three more of the *St Vincent* class (*Collingwood*, *St Vincent* and *Vanguard*), launched between 7 November 1908 and 22 February 1909, with all completed and in service by April 1910. Considering that these were laid down between February 1907 and April 1908, it is evident that the British shipyards were getting into the swing of producing dreadnoughts at breathtaking speed. The principal builders for these craft were Portsmouth Dockyard, Devonport Dockyard, Vickers at Barrow-in-Furness and Elswick in Tyneside. Although in most ways the *St Vincent* class replicated the previous dreadnought vessels, there were some important changes. The biggest was a change in the armament. The main guns on the previous dreadnoughts – the 45-calibre-long Mk X guns – were replaced with the 50-calibre Mk XI guns, the new guns theoretically offering increased muzzle velocity and therefore a greater range and flatter trajectory. As I point out in Chapter 3, these benefits were not realised fully in reality. Moreover, the addition of the longer, heavier guns meant that the ship had to be stretched in length by about 10ft (to 536ft overall), with a slight increase in beam and a slight decrease in draught. Also, while the *Bellerophon* class had a displacement of 18,600 tons, the *St Vincent* vessels were

at 19,700 tons (normal load). Not only was the weight of the vessel increased by the modifications in the main armament, but the warship also had an additional four 4in QF guns, making a total of 20. Two of these guns were removed by 1916: those mounted atop 'A' and 'B' turrets.

Following *Dreadnought*, the *Bellerophon* and *St Vincent* classes of warship had brought little substantial change to the overall layout of the new British battleship. Herein lay a risk, particularly in the configuration of the armament. The British had watched with interest as the Americans produced their *South Carolina* class of dreadnoughts, the lead ship of the class laid down on 18 December 1906 and completed on 1 March 1910. What made the *South Carolina* truly notable was that it was the first battleship with superfiring turrets both fore and aft – the innermost turret of each pair was raised so that it could fire directly over the top of the turret in front. This invention, courtesy of Chief Constructor Washington L. Capps, transformed battleship firepower. Not only were there space savings to be had from the design, but it also meant that four guns (the *South Carolina* had 8 × 12in guns set in turreted pairs) could engage targets directly ahead or behind at the same time, or all eight guns could be swivelled to deliver a full broadside.

Neptune and the *Colossus* class

The British sat up and took notice, but at first only partially with the development and launch of HMS *Neptune*. Actually, the British were already getting some experience of building battleships with superfiring turrets. A Brazilian order for two dreadnought-type battleships, designed to counter Argentinian naval expansions, featured superfiring turrets fore and aft, plus the usual wing turrets of the earlier British dreadnoughts. This order, fulfilled by Armstrong and Vickers, gave the British a technical

OVERLEAF Here are three deck plans for HMS *St Vincent* – from top to bottom: flying deck, main deck and middle deck. Compared to the *Bellerophon* class, the space between 'X' and 'Y' turrets was stretched by 10ft. *(NMM)*

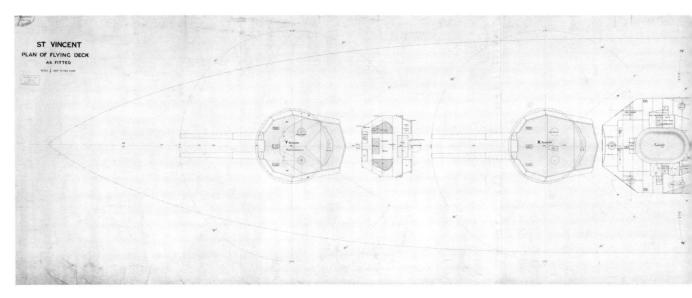

ST VINCENT
PLAN OF FLYING DECK
AS FITTED

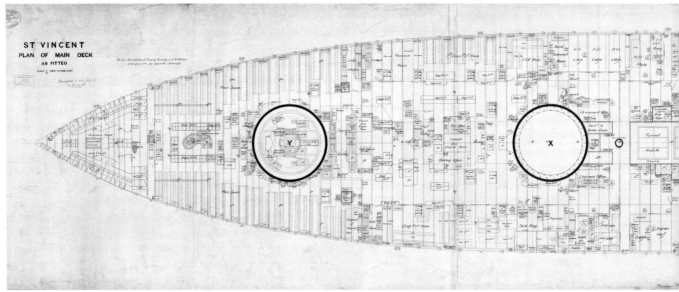

ST VINCENT
PLAN OF MAIN DECK
AS FITTED

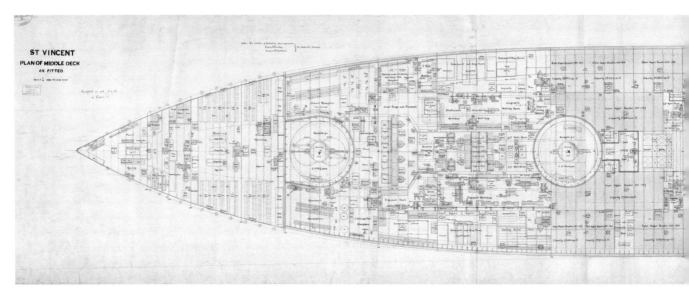

ST VINCENT
PLAN OF MIDDLE DECK
AS FITTED

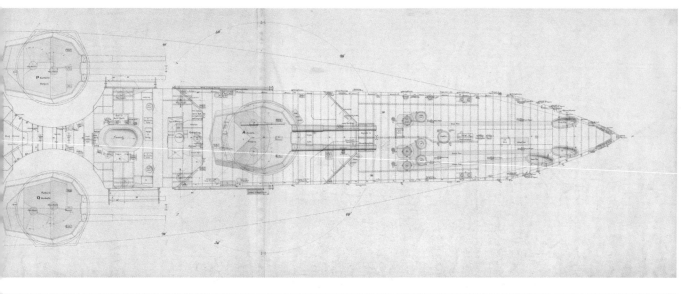

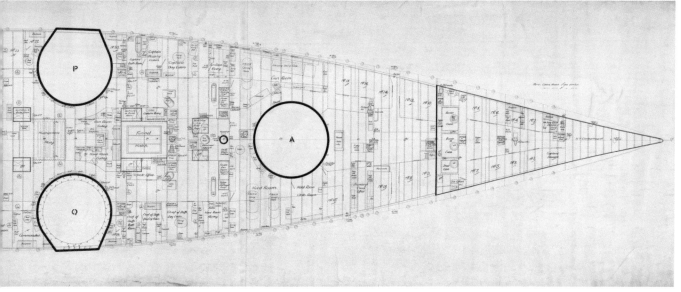

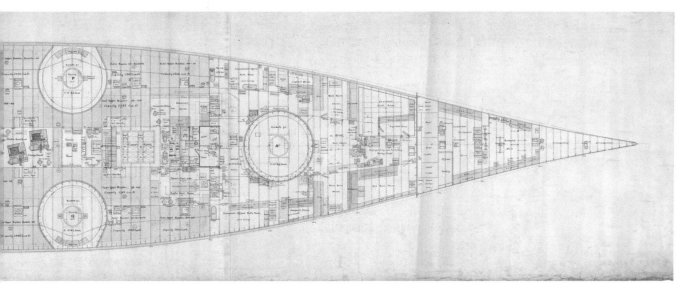

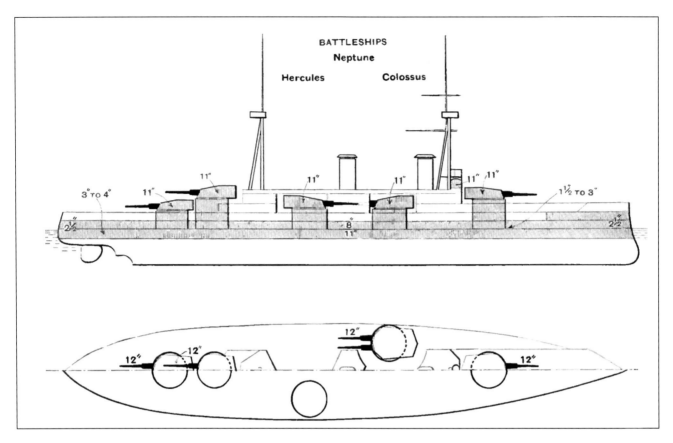

BATTLESHIPS
Neptune
Hercules   Colossus

ABOVE This basic plan of the *Colossus*-class ships illustrates how the gunnery configuration enabled a full broadside, even with guns on the beam.

understanding of the superfiring configuration, which they then applied to *Neptune*.

Neptune was laid down on 19 January 1909, launched on 30 September 1909, and completed in January 1911. The layout of the main guns, and by consequence the superstructure, was radically different. The ten 12in guns, paired in turrets, were arranged thus: a single turret which sat at the front of the ship, while at the rear there were two turrets, one superfiring over the other. But the British had also decided to do something about the limited traverse of the wing turrets. On *Neptune*, these turrets were offset in relation to each other, and the bridge deck was set on raised platforms, the gap beneath each platform allowing the port wing turret to turn and be trained directly starboard, and vice versa. What this meant was that the *Neptune* could, if a target was directly to broadside, fire all ten guns at the same target at the same time.

Neptune was, in reality, something of a botched job. While theoretically she had broadside firepower far greater than anything else on the seas at the time, the reality was that using the wing turrets to fire across deck was a direct route to superstructure damage. However,

Neptune included some actual improvements. The ship was fitted with four cruising turbines, which enhanced performance and economy at lower speeds, plus the ship received upgraded armour below the waterline. Later in its career, *Neptune* also became the first battleship to be fitted with gunnery control equipment on a platform beneath the foremast main top. Additionally, it addressed the problem of smoke from the forward funnel clouding the manned mast positions by fitting an inclined cowl.

Hot on the heels of *Neptune* were the *Colossus* class of dreadnoughts, consisting of *Colossus* (completed July 1911) and *Hercules* (completed August 1911). These were essentially of the same design as *Neptune*, but with some tweaks, not all with the backing of logic, it seems. The class kept the same gunnery configuration as *Neptune*, albeit with the 'P' and 'Q' wing turrets slightly closer together to give more room for the forward and aft superstructure. The most noticeable change was that the foremast was moved to behind the forward funnel, as part of a weight-saving initiative. Unfortunately, this only increased the problem of smoke swirling around the foretop, and the bridge also became polluted.

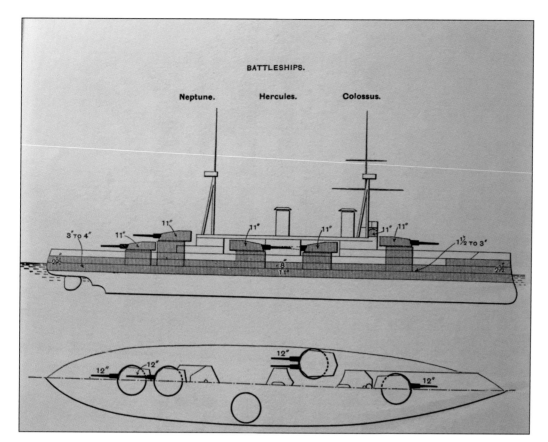

BATTLESHIPS.

Neptune.   Hercules.   Colossus.

LEFT In this 1913 illustration we see the turret arrangement for the *Neptune* and *Colossus* class vessels that enabled the ship to fire a full ten-gun broadside.

There were some other, less visible, changes to the *Colossus* class. Admiralty insistence on improved armour around the guns meant that armour was trimmed off the stern and bow belt sections. The ship was now fitted with 21in torpedo tubes rather than the previous 18in varieties.

Note that in some ways we are now nearing the end of the dreadnought story, because the Admiralty was gravitating towards the super dreadnought ships, which is expanded upon later in this chapter. But there was one final development in the story of dreadnoughts proper – HMS *Agincourt*. As the arms race between Brazil and Argentina escalated, Brazil commissioned a third dreadnought from Britain, to be called the *Rio de Janeiro*. The Brazilians evidently intended the ship to be the ultimate expression of firepower, as it was armed with no fewer than 14 x 12in guns. What was striking was that all of these guns were mounted on the centreline of the ship, with superfiring pairs of turrets fore and aft, a back-to-back pair amidships, plus an additional turret aft, between 'Y' turret and the superstructure. With an overall length of 671ft 6in and a

displacement of more than 32,000 tons fully laden, *Agincourt* was a mighty addition to any fleet. And it so happened that the fleet would be British. Financial problems meant that the Brazilians eventually had to sell the warship to the Turkish government even before it had left the Armstrong Whitworth shipyard. With the outbreak of war in 1914, however, there was concern that the warship might go to a country that was about to become an enemy; when this indeed proved to be the case, *Agincourt* went into the British arsenal.

BELOW This revealing image shows how coal storage could also act as an integral part of the ship's protection, the coal bunkers shielding vital inner engineering spaces. (NMRN)

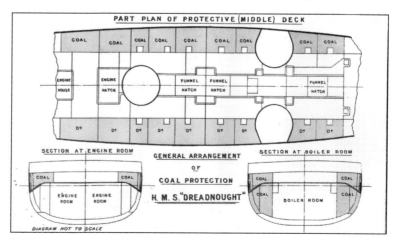

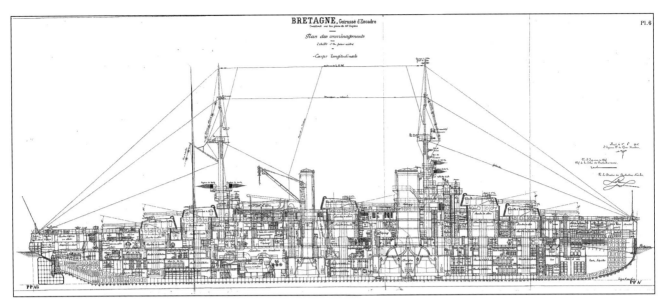

BRETAGNE, Cuirassé d'Escadre

Pl.6

ABOVE A very detailed plan of *Bretagne*, the lead ship of three super dreadnoughts built for the French Navy between 1912 and 1916.

The super dreadnoughts

One of the main factors determining the layout of the super dreadnoughts was obviously the fitting of the new, heavier 13.5in armament. With the superfiring turrets already a proven concept, all the super dreadnoughts would have the guns arranged on the centreline; placing any guns on the wings would have adversely affected stability.

The first of the super dreadnoughts was the *Orion* class, consisting of four vessels – *Conqueror*, *Monarch*, *Orion* and *Thunderer*. The gun arrangement for these ships was as follows: superfiring pairs of twin-gun turrets fore and aft, and a single turret amidships just behind the boat deck, giving a maximum broadside of 10 guns. The ship was heavier, at 22,500 tons displacement, than the previous dreadnoughts, and it was not just the guns that were adding to the weight. Armoured protection was also improved, with side armour covering the full depth of the hull and also reaching a maximum depth of 12in. The forward mast remained behind the forward funnel, and as the foremast became increasingly important in the gunnery role, with more equipment fitted up in the foretop, both the mast and the funnel became the subject of modifications to improve clearance from smoke, especially during the war years.

The main gun layout of the *Orion* class was essentially repeated in the next two classes of super dreadnought – the *King George V*

class (*King George V*, *Centurion*, *Audacious* and *Ajax*) and the *Iron Duke* class (*Iron Duke*, *Marlborough*, *Benbow* and *Emperor of India*). Yet some adjustments were made to other areas of the design, to make an advance over the capabilities of the *Orion*-class ships. Their dimensions were slightly increased – overall length was 597ft 6in and beam was 89ft. More significant changes related to the secondary armament and the foremast. Regarding the former, the *King George V*-class ships each had 16 × 4in QF guns in single mounts. Twelve of these were concentrated in the front half of the ship, as experience proved that when attempting to defeat attacks from torpedo boats, the firepower forward was far more important than the firepower aft. Each 4in gun position was also provided with 3in armour protection. With the *King George V* class, the foremast was also located in front of the forward funnel, a far more satisfactory arrangement.

The four ships of the *Iron Duke* class were part of the 1911 naval programme, being laid down in January and May 2012 and coming into service in the winter of 1913. Again, it was the secondary armament that formed the principal change from previous ships, as the concept of the all-big-gun warship began to wane. The *Iron Duke*-class warships mounted 12 × 6in Mk VII BL guns in single mounts around the ship, again with the bulk of the firepower concentrated forward. Unlike earlier vessels, however, the 6in guns were set below the main deck level, projecting out of the hull, with one pair of guns set in scalloped recesses in the hull below 'Y' turret (Konstam, *British Battleships 1914–18 – The Super Dreadnoughts*, 2013, p. 14). A problem, which one imagines should have been foreseen, was that the gun positions became flooded with seawater in rough conditions, a situation that involved building protective structures around most of the guns, and relocating the guns under 'Y' turret to a position under the bridge.

The *Iron Duke* class were, again, larger ships than their predecessors, with an overall length of 622ft 9in and a beam of 90ft. The tripod foremast, now heavier and more substantial and with a larger control top, had improved clearance from the funnel smoke, and the funnels themselves were redesigned with more slender outlines.

Although the *Orion*, *King George V* and *Iron Duke* classes made constant evolutionary steps, it was with the *Queen Elizabeth* class that the super dreadnoughts took more of a leap into the future. The class was produced in response to news that foreign nations were investing in installing guns of calibres exceeding 13.5in. Furthermore, improvements in propulsion meant that the next generation of British warship had to bring the capability of greater speed to the table. Thus Sir Philip Watts and his team set to work again, this time with the objective of incorporating a 15in gun main armament. It would be Watts's final, and arguably most impressive, of the dreadnought designs.

The *Queen Elizabeth* class was built between October 1912 and February 1916. Most critical of the many differences in this

class was the installation of eight 15in guns, with two superfiring turrets fore and aft – no further main guns were installed amidships, although this had been seriously considered during the proposal stages. The reduction in the number of guns was ostensibly offset by the weight of shell the battleships could throw out, by virtue of the larger calibre. The secondary armament consisted of 16 hull-mounted 6in guns, although this number was reduced when it was discovered that the four guns mounted in the stern were constantly struggling with seawater inundation.

As a result, the *Queen Elizabeth* vessels had a considerable surge in firepower. But the signal changes did not stop there. This class of ships was the first in the Royal Navy to switch purely to oil-fired engines, dispensing with coal altogether. The engines were arranged in two sections, with protective bulkheads separating the groupings. High-pressure turbines were set to power the outer two of the four shafts,

ABOVE HMS *Iron Duke* **under steam, sailing out of Portsmouth in 1914 minus her torpedo nets.**

BELOW HMS *Agincourt*, **in the foreground, sits alongside other capital ships of the Royal Navy at Scapa Flow in 1918.** *(US Navy)*

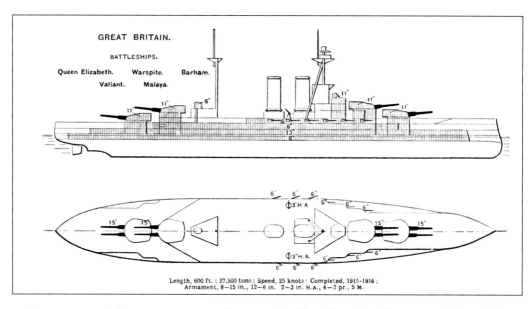

GREAT BRITAIN.

BATTLESHIPS.

Queen Elizabeth.   Warspite.   Barham.
Valiant.   Malaya.

Length, 600 ft. ; 27,500 tons ; Speed, 25 knots : Completed, 1915-1916 ;
Armament, 8—15 in., 12—6 in. 2—3 in. H.A., 4—3 pr., 5 M.

and low-pressure turbines were connected to the inner shafts. The oil fuel was stored in enormous bunkers, 30ft high, alongside the boiler rooms.

The *Queen Elizabeth* was the first of a new class of 'fast battleships' – they could make 23 knots at full speed. With their impressive firepower and swift legs, these ships laid down something of a challenge to Eustace Tennyson d'Eyncourt, the new DNC, as he stepped into the shoes of the now legendary Watts. For the 1913 estimates, d'Eyncourt had to respond to an Admiralty which wanted the next generation of battleships to be equipped with no fewer than 10 × 15in guns. D'Eyncourt attempted this design from several different angles, including having five twin turrets and also using some triple-gun turrets, but he largely resisted the proposition, on the grounds of its effect on displacement and the general stability of the ship. So in the end the five ships (*Royal Sovereign*,

Ramillies, *Resolution*, *Revenge* and *Royal Oak*) of the *Royal Sovereign* class retained the eight-gun, four-turret arrangement. Yet the ships were different from their predecessors in several key ways. For a start, they were more compact – the overall length of the *Royal Sovereign* vessels was around 580ft 7in, a full 20ft shorter than the *Queen Elizabeth* warships, although displacement was roughly the same. The weight of the ship was increased by a uniform belt of 13in armour along the middle and lower sides amidships; the *Queen Elizabeth* ships also had a 13in armour section, but this was in a tapering arrangement, dropping to 8in thickness just below the waterline. The *Royal Sovereign* ships were also fitted with underwater 'torpedo bulges' – protective swellings against the side of the ships' hulls some 220ft long and 7ft 3in wide. The interior of each bulge was composed of watertight compartments and sections of tightly packed hollow tubes. The whole structure was designed to soak up some of the blast effect of a torpedo or mine strike, hopefully preserving the integrity of the main hull. The torpedo bulges were not an integral part of the original design; they were added on during the construction process after naval tests suggested their value. (Note that *Revenge* and *Resolution* were fitted with an improved version of this defensive feature, without the internal tubes.)

There were other notable features of the *Royal Sovereign* class, which together should suffice to resist the pejorative label of 'cut-price *Queen Elizabeths*' that they garnered from

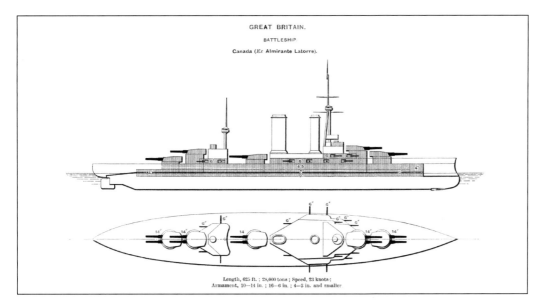

GREAT BRITAIN.

BATTLESHIP.

Canada (Ex Almirante Latorre).

Length, 625 ft. ; 28,000 tons ; Speed, 23 knots ;
Armament, 10—14 in. ; 16—6 in. ; 4—3 in. and smaller.

LEFT A plan of
HMS *Canada* from
1915, with 6in guns
clustered thickly
around the forward
superstructure.

some contemporaries. The 14 × 6in guns that comprised the secondary armament were set back more amidships, to avoid the flooding problems of the gunnery positions of earlier classes. The ships' metacentric height was lowered, to enhance the steadiness required for accurate shooting. A notable feature of the superstructure was that there was only one funnel, with the high foretop well out of the reach of the funnel's smoke emissions.

Two more individual vessels require some consideration before we complete our overview of the dreadnoughts and super dreadnoughts. These were HMS *Erin* and HMS *Canada*. The battleship *Erin* began life as another privately built warship, constructed by Vickers for the Turkish government just before the onset of the First World War. Initially named *Reshad V*, then (from 1913) *Reshadieh*, the warship eventually became HMS *Erin* when the Turks allied themselves with the Central Powers in August 1914.

Erin was a striking vessel, similar to the *Orion* class but slightly smaller. She was formidably well armed, with 10 × 13.5in guns – two pairs of superfiring turrets fore and aft, plus another turret set on the centreline amidships. She also had a secondary battery of 16 × 6in guns, meaning that she was a seriously well-armed warship. Although the vessel was originally designed with two tripod masts, this configuration was scaled down to one large tripod mast at the front plus a single-pole mainmast for the radio aerials. However, by the time the ship entered British service the mainmast had gone altogether;

now just a single tripod foremast sat in front of two closely arranged funnels. Although *Erin* had a mixed reception from its crews – the accommodation arrangements were especially cramped for both officers and men alike – she was a serviceable, fast and effective addition to the Royal Navy's arsenal.

HMS *Canada* was another privately built vessel that was war purchased into the Royal Navy. This time the original customer was Chile, keen to keep up with the South American naval arms race that was every bit as heated as the one happening across the Atlantic in Europe. The ship was called *Almirante Latorre*, and was one of a pair of Chilean dreadnoughts under construction in British shipyards, although she was the only one completed by the outbreak of war in 1914, when she was taken over by the Royal Navy. Like *Erin*, *Canada* packed a punch – she had a main armament of ten 14in guns (the only British warship to carry 14in guns during the First World War), plus a secondary armament of 16 × 6in guns. It was not as well armoured, however, as some of the other super dreadnoughts around at this time.

The *Royal Sovereign* class was the last of the major classes of super dreadnoughts to be produced. As we shall see in later chapters, the changing conditions of naval warfare altered the future of the battleship brand itself. Yet within a certain spectrum of design objectives, principally those of producing fast, heavily armed warships, the dreadnoughts and super dreadnoughts had been a success.

Chapter Three

Firepower

The raison d'être of the dreadnoughts was firepower. This was not just a matter of calibre, range and explosive force; a dreadnought's guns had to be integrated with a fast, efficient and accurate system of fire control.

OPPOSITE 'Togo', one of several pets to grace the decks of HMS *Dreadnought*, perches atop the barrel of a 12in main gun. *(NMRN)*

ABOVE *Dreadnought* fires the guns of its aft turret. Here we can see that the 12-pdrs are still mounted atop the turret roofs, though they were later removed. *(NMRN)*

BELOW *Dreadnought*'s 'Q' turret is fired during gunnery trials. Smoke obscuration was a key reason why battleships adopted centralised and elevated fire-control platforms. *(NMRN)*

The dreadnoughts were in many ways only made a viable concept because of the complex changes in naval gun design and fire control by the beginning of the 20th century. The most critical of all these changes was the introduction of effective naval breech-loading mechanisms during the mid-19th century. Breech-loaders not only allowed the loading of more powerful charges, they also permitted gun barrels to be longer, by virtue of the fact that the gun didn't need to be withdrawn back into the ship for muzzle loading. Longer barrels meant increased velocities and therefore improved range, penetration and weight of shot, which were deciding factors in an age of iron-clad enemies. A seminal advance came with the French invention, around 1845, of the interrupted screw breech system, which enabled a rapid

means of loading plus, when combined with an appropriate chamber thickness, a secure means of locking against the massive pressures of detonation. The interrupted screw became one of the principal (although not the only) locking mechanisms for heavy guns, while sliding breech blocks were more common on lighter weapons, especially those that utilised that other major advance of the 19th century – the unitary metallic-cased shell.

Of course it was one matter to load and fire a gun, but it was another altogether to move that gun smoothly and quickly on to the correct bearing and elevation. Yet the technologies of gun mount had also seen major progress by the time that *Dreadnought* was laid down. Hydraulic power, invented at the very end of the 18th century initially for its applications to factory machinery, made its way into naval gun machinery by the second half of the 19th century, providing a smooth, quiet and reliable system for training the guns. The hydraulic medium was either fresh water (in some systems salt water could be drawn in if there was a sudden critical loss of hydraulic fluid) or oil; water was the preferred fluid used in British guns. Hydraulic systems were also better suited to the rapid back-and-forth training movements required in battle, and were especially more resilient under the repeated changes of direction fed from mechanised fire-control systems; a true revolution in naval gunnery.

Then there was the matter of protection for the gun crews. While secondary armaments might be exposed deck guns, the main guns and their operators were too important to leave unprotected. This was where turrets and barbettes had their role. (The differences between the two are explored in the feature box 'Turret and barbette'.) From the mid-19th century, guns were increasingly emplaced in turrets/barbettes mounted either on the deck or set into the hull structure. From the 1870s twin-gun turrets also became more common.

The combination of hydraulically powered turrets, barbettes and mounts, plus the constant improvements in breech-loading gun technology and in the shells themselves, led to the mighty firepower of the dreadnoughts and super dreadnoughts, guns that shook the foundations of global politics as much as they rippled the surface of the oceans.

TURRET AND BARBETTE

There is frequently confusion over the distinction between turrets and barbettes.

The uncertainty has arisen because in many ways the separation between the two ceased to be watertight, at least in appearance. Essentially a barbette consists of a fixed protective armoured ring, in which the gun sits and rotates. A turret, by contrast, is a fully armoured housing that rotates in its entirety with the gun. The advantage of the barbette is that the machinery required to move the gun does not have to be as powerful as that of a turret. However, barbettes often do not offer the high degree of protection afforded by a turret. Yet, in the late 19th century, barbette designs were improved with the addition of an enclosing armoured gun house that rotated with the guns. These types of structures also became known as turrets. Strictly speaking, *Dreadnought* was fitted with barbettes, but turret is used as a more familiar term.

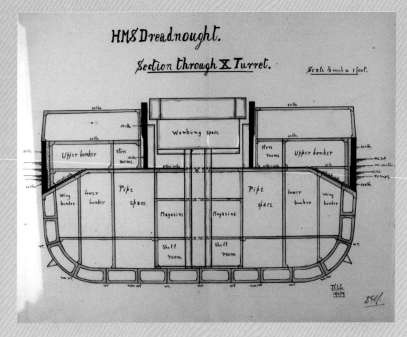

ABOVE This useful cross-section diagram shows the arrangement of shell rooms and magazines around the ammunition hoist trunking, feeding up the turret working space. *(NMRN)*

12in main guns and mounts

The main gun that graced the decks of the *Dreadnought* plus the *Bellerophon* class (also the preceding *Lord Nelson* class of pre-dreadnought and the contemporary *Invincible* and *Indefatigable* classes of battlecruiser) was the BL (breech-loading) 12in Mk X 45-calibre. With a total length of 557.5in and weighing 56 tons, this was a substantial piece of weaponry. The breech was of the Wellin interrupted-screw type, and the barrel was of a wire-wound construction, meaning that layers of steel ribbon wire were wrapped around the inner liner (which formed the bore and held the rifling), with each layer of wire having a different tension. The wire-wound gun was the preferred method of construction by many naval weapon builders at this time, as it gave a great tangential strength to the gun barrel. Some nations, especially the United States, preferred the 'built-up method', made up from composite layers of forged steel, the Americans being of the opinion that this method's longitudinal strength meant avoiding the barrel droop sometimes experienced by well-worn wire-wound guns. The Mk X had a

polygroove rifling system at a rate of one turn in every 30 calibres. Firing an 850lb shell propelled by 258lb bags of MD cordite, the gun could generate muzzle velocities of around 2,800ft/sec, giving a maximum range of 16,400yd.

BELOW Officers and men gather beneath 'Q' turret aboard *Dreadnought*. The 12-pdr guns on top were fitted on pedestal mounts; the mounts on the turret roofs had no traverse stops. *(NMRN)*

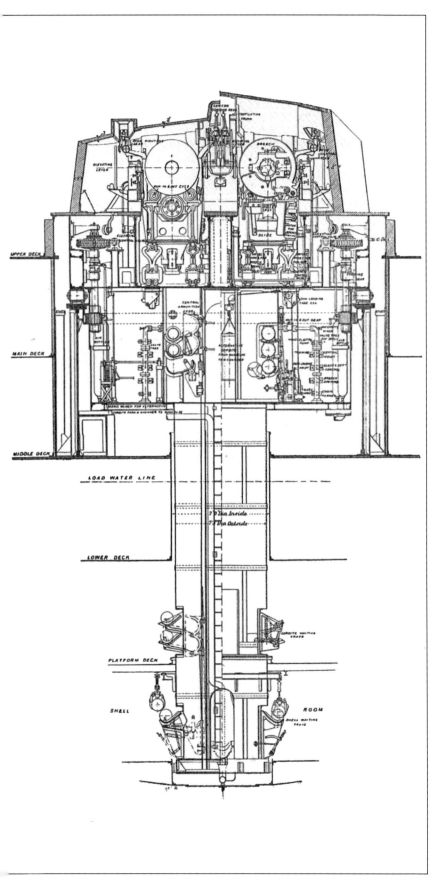

On *Dreadnought* itself, the Mk X gun was set on a BVIII (Vickers) mounting. On direction from the fire-control centre, shells and cordite charges were conveyed from the shell rooms and magazines via hoists running up through central trunking. The shell components were transferred into gunloading cages corresponding to each barrel, and were then hydraulically rammed into the open breech, which was closed for firing. The automation meant that the rate of fire was roughly two shells every minute, depending on the efficiency of the fire-control system.

The 12in gun was the standard weapon for dreadnought battleships through the *Bellerophon*, *St Vincent* and *Colossus* classes, plus the individual battleships *Neptune* and *Agincourt*. There was some evolution in both gun and mounting within this calibre, however. *Neptune*, as well as the *St Vincent* and *Colossus* classes, took the Mk XI gun, which was 50 calibres in length, the additional length squeezing up the muzzle velocity and the overall range to 21,000yd. The gun could also take a heavier individual powder charge (306lb). The mounting for the Mk XI in these vessels was the BXI for all but the *Hercules*, which had the BXII mounting. These mountings benefited from swashplate training engines, which gave a smoother and steadier turning movement, and were therefore more easily controlled during an engagement.

Before moving on to heavier calibres, we should also note the 12in guns fitted to *Agincourt*. These were of the Mk XIII type, of 45 calibres and were installed on a special mounting made by the Elswick company.

As noted in the previous two chapters, the 12in guns of the dreadnoughts progressively gave way to guns of larger calibre and greater destructive force, mounted in the new generations of super dreadnought. Peter Hodges, in his book *The Big Gun: Battleship Main Armament 1860–1945*, explains some

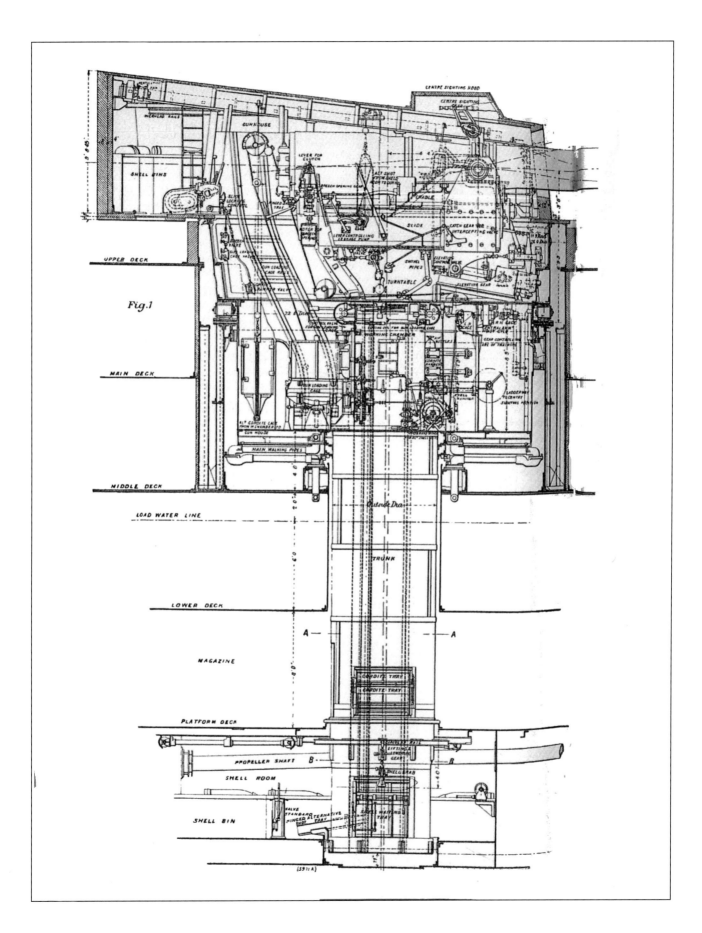

Fig.1

THE DREADNOUGHT STEAMING AND CLEARED FOR ACTION. SHE IS SEEN TURNING.

H.I.J.M.S "MIKASA".
GENERAL ARRANGEMENT OF TURRET AND MOUNTING FOR A PAIR OF 12 INCH 49 TON B.L GUNS.

SECTIONAL ELEVATION
40 Calibre Guns.

of the issues affecting the 12in guns of the dreadnought era:

> *The problems of smooth mounting control in elevation and training during the 12in era were quite severe. The single-lever control linkages introduced considerable backlash, and were finally abandoned in the later classes in favour of a wheel control. The old 3-cylinder oscillating training engines were superseded for a short time by the Elswick-designed 6-cylinder unit but, with the advent of the very efficient swashplate machine, together with finer tolerance control valves, a 'sweetness' of control was finally achieved.*

Such mechanical improvements were part of a never-ending process of improving and enhancing the dreadnought gunnery systems, and there was a constant process of self-criticism in place. This was evident during *Dreadnought*'s Experimental Cruise, the report from which included a long section entitled 'Suggested Gunnery Improvements', consisting of a total of 39 points. Some select points are worth quoting, to reveal the type of issues that emerged.

> *25) The elevating gear of the 12-in. guns requires improving.*
> *27) At present the 12-in. sights vibrate a great deal while either 12-in. gun is being loaded, absolutely preventing the guns being laid during the loading operations. This can be rectified by making the steel rod carrying the telescope sleeve more rigid, since no vibration can be traced in the connection below the rod.*
> *29) Fire control and gun firing switchboard should be moved from 'X' space and placed*

LEFT A diagram of the Elswick 12in guns and machinery for the Japanese battleship *Mikasa*, the illustration suggesting the journey of a shell from shell room to gun breech.

RIGHT This interesting diagram from *The Navy Annual 1913* shows the layouts of some competing German battleships, including *Nassau*, the first German dreadnought. Maximum broadside of the *Nassau* was eight 11in guns.

in 'A' space near exchange, as this would be much cooler, and does not sweat so much at sea.

31) A small hand lift pump, about 2-in. in diameter, with a 6-ft flexible suction, should be provided for pumping out the water in the bottom of the 12-in. shell-bays when they are full of shell. At present there is no means of doing this except by shifting all the shell.

38) The main transmitting station should be shifted down one deck to the compartment immediately below its present position, it would then be below the armour deck.

39) The main shell and cordite hoists in 'A' turret should be made to work quicker.

Report on Experimental Cruise, *1907*

This selection of issues, plus the others in the list (not reproduced here), is a mixture of the annoying (such as the water-filled shell bays) and the profound. Some of these problems would be dealt with during the successive development stages of the 12in guns, while others would be addressed in later guns with wider bores.

Larger-calibre guns and mounts

The first of the British big guns beyond 12in was the 13.5in Mk V, as mounted in some ships of the *Orion*, *King George V* and *Iron Duke* classes. This piece of firepower was a substantial increase in size, weight and potential force over the preceding guns. The barrel now measured 625.9in and weighed 76 tons. The weight of the 13.5in shell was either 1,250lb or 1,400lb, depending on shell type, but the weight of charge was, thanks to improved propellant, only 293lb. Nevertheless it added

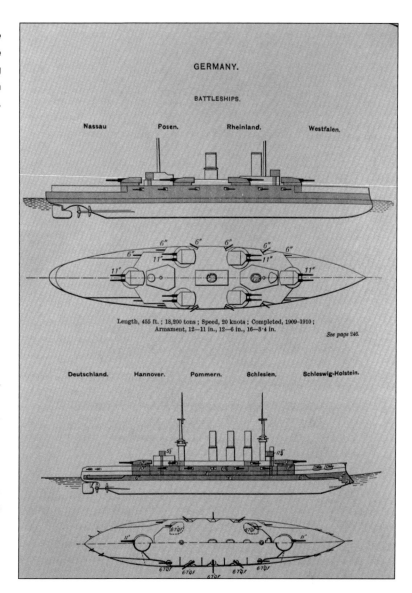

GERMANY.

BATTLESHIPS.

Nassau.   Posen.   Rheinland.   Westfalen.

Length, 455 ft. ; 18,200 tons ; Speed, 20 knots ; Completed, 1909–1910 ;
Armament, 12—11 in., 12—6 in., 16—8·4 in.

See page 246.

Deutschland.   Hannover.   Pommern.   Schlesien.   Schleswig-Holstein.

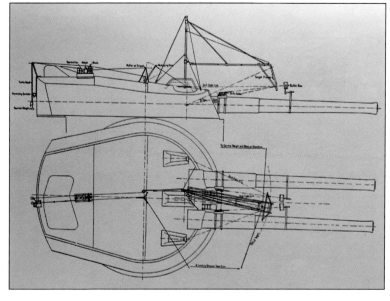

RIGHT A diagram showing a deflection teaching device fitted to a pair of Armstrong 14in guns.

ABOVE The challenge of delivering an effective broadside was to ensure that the guns were each trained on the target, and not simply working in parallel with one another.

BELOW This simplified diagram from *The Wonder Book of the Navy* (4th edition) in the 1920s usefully illustrates gunnery procedures and spaces.

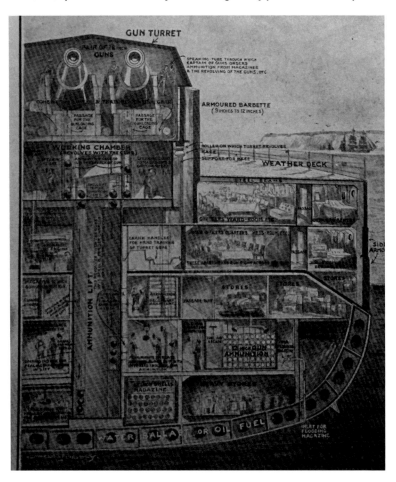

an additional 2,000yd of maximum range in comparison with the Mk XI.

Some significant design work took place to incorporate the 13.5in guns (which measured 625.9in) into gunhouse and trunk dimensions that were actually identical to those in the Mk XI. The trunking supply system for the cordite and the shells had to be reconfigured, as did some of the layout and operating procedures in the working chamber (the space in which the shells were readied for loading). The working chamber featured shell storage space for six rounds per gun, while the gunhouse space had room for eight rounds per gun. Note also that there were some electromechanical improvements to the mounting, such as the fitting of a Pelton wheel turbo-generator to provide power to the firing circuits.

While *Conqueror*, *Ajax* and *Benbow* were all equipped with the Mk V 13.5in gun, they had new Mk III mounts produced by Coventry Ordnance Works, rather than Vickers or Elswick. There were many differences between these and the other mounts, including:

- Different configuration of the elevation piston and cylinder (the elevating cylinder was pivoted to allow the gun to go through its full range of depression and elevation)
- 7-cylinder reciprocating training engines (as opposed to the swashplate type)
- Curved gunhouse side plates
- Differences in the mechanisms for hoisting and loading shells and propellant bags.

Peter Hodges' book notes that the 'ammunition supply arrangements conceived by the Coventry works were peculiar and are, perhaps, indicative of their experience in such matters' (p. 64). However, the 13.5in mountings also reflected those of the later 15in weapons, so their functionality was obviously serviceable.

The next step up in the Royal Navy's calibre race was the 14in guns mounted in one particular ship, HMS *Canada*. The guns were 14in Mk I 45-calibre weapons, set in twin Mk I mountings. The statistics show an inexorable drift upwards when compared to previous guns. The barrel length had extended to 648.4in, with a commensurate increase in weight to 85 tons. The rifling inside the gun's bore retained the same pattern of twist – one turn in every

SHELL-LOADING PROCEDURE

Across the dreadnoughts and super dreadnoughts, there were numerous different mechanical arrangements for transferring shells and cordite bags to the ship's main guns. However, there were some general principles of operation. The 12in shells were stored deep down in the ship, below the waterline, in shell rooms, with the corresponding propellant bags being held in the nearby magazines, usually located above the shell rooms. The shell rooms, magazines and handling rooms (spaces for preparing the propellant for delivery to the turret) would be positioned around a central ammunition lift, which contained hoists and unitary (typical in British designs) or separate cages for lifting the ammunition components straight up to the turret directly above. One hoist or set of hoists would serve each gun. A 'working chamber' sat directly beneath the rotating turret structure – note that the working chamber plus the lifting trunk all rotated in sympathy with the turret, to ensure alignment of the hoists with the guns. Also note that flashproof doors and scuttles were fitted into the trunk and other positions along the path of ammunition travel, these closing after the movement of ammunition to ensure that there was no direct passage for flame to move between the deck/turret and the magazines, should the upper parts of the ship be hit by enemy shellfire. The occupants of the working chamber could also communicate, via voice pipe, directly with the personnel in the shell rooms and handling rooms below. From the handling rooms, shells and propellant bags would be placed into the hoist cages (the heavy shells were lifted by a hydraulic grab) and raised to the working chamber, which also held some ready ammunition in case the hydraulics for the trunk failed for some reason. When the guns were ready to fire, the ammunition would be lifted via a gun-loading cage to the turret, where each component was aligned with the breech and loaded into place by telescopic rammers. The breech could now be closed and the gun fired.

30 calibres – as the 12in and 13.5in guns, the only difference being that the increased length of barrel raised the number of grooves to 84 (the 13.5in gun had 68 grooves). The muzzle velocity rose fractionally to 2,507ft/sec, with a maximum range of 24,300yd.

The apogee of the super dreadnought guns was of course the 15in BL Mk I gun set in the twin Mk I mounting. Including the breech, each of these mighty guns weighed 100 tons. Taken together, the twin guns and the entire mounting structure weighed a colossal 750 tons, giving an indication of how armament constituted a high percentage of a battleship's final weight. If four 428lb quarter charges (a 'full charge') were used to fire the 1,920lb shell, the resulting energy generated was sufficient to lift a weight of 84,000 tons a height of 1ft into the air. Another wide-eyed contemporary also noted that if 51in of solid steel were added to the end of the muzzle, the shell would still pass right through it (although obviously it would be best for this theory to remain untested). Maximum range for the gun was 23,734yd at a full elevation of 20° (the range of elevation was +20° to -5° in the Mk I mounting). The gunhouse was protected by extremely substantial armour, to a depth of 13in on the front face, 11in around the sides and at the rear and 5in on the roof.

The big guns of the dreadnoughts and the super dreadnoughts were truly formidable examples of naval technology. Because of the rationale of the all-big-gun battleship, they

ABOVE Observation balloons could be useful assets for both reconnaissance and for long-range target-spotting and gunnery adjustment.

The shells may have been light and the range comparatively short, but the 12-pdr guns made up for these deficiencies with excellent rates of fire, of about 20rpm in the hands of a proficient crew. For this reason, they were primarily intended as anti-torpedo boat armament, although with the elevation tipped up dramatically they could also be applied as anti-aircraft weapons. (Note that the 12-pdr had originally been intended as an anti-destroyer weapon, but this purpose had been abandoned in 1906 after trials found it wanting in this regard, especially when compared to the 4in gun.)

The 12-pdr's P.IV* mounting was obviously critical to the gun's fast-response and quick-firing role. Here an official Royal Navy document explains some of the details of this mount:

The 12-pr. 18-cwt guns are on P.IV* mountings, each fitted with two cross-connected telescopic sights, for which two V.P. 5–12 day and night telescopes are supplied. Each mounting has a training wheel on the right, and elevating wheel on the left. The guns are fitted for dynamo firing, the main circuit lead to the dynamo being a permanent one, but the leads of the auxiliary circuits above the lower deck are flexible and are kept stowed below during the day action. The combined range and deflection receivers and fire-gongs and their cables are also kept below under protection.

One critical role of the 12-pdr guns was that of repelling a surprise night attack, as with ready ammunition it would take a matter of seconds to bring a gun into action, as

are also the weapons that garner the most attention. Yet the 'all-big-gun' label is something of a misnomer, for these battleships were bristling with a spectrum of other armament, of not inconsiderable power.

Secondary armament

Looking back to the original *Dreadnought*, the principal element of the secondary armament was 24 × QF 12-pdr 18cwt guns, each set in a single mount. Compared to its much bigger brothers gracing the main turrets, the 12-pdr guns were diminutive indeed. They weighed 18cwt (2,016lb) and had an overall length of 154.7in, including a chamber length of 20.18in. The gun fired 3in shells each weighing 12.5lb, with gyroscopic stability imparted by 20 rifling grooves with a 1/30 twist rate. The muzzle velocity was 2,660ft/sec with an effective range of 9,300yd at +20° elevation.

opposed to minutes for the main guns. (At close ranges, furthermore, the main guns would have a limited utility.) For this reason, the ship was heavily fitted with searchlight systems, which were tactically and practically integrated into the fire-control system. The previously quoted naval document explains the configuration of these searchlights:

Twelve 36-in. searchlight projectors are mounted. Each of these is allotted an arc of 30°, and all 12 lights are controlled from the top of the fore chart-house, where they are under the captain's immediate supervision. Alternative positions for controlling them are on the main control position and after signal tower for the foremost and after lights respectively.

Four of the searchlights (Ns. 2 and 5 each side) have their training and elevation electrically controlled by means of levers on top of fore chart-house, and can also be switched on or off from there. The remaining eight are elevated and trained by hand at the

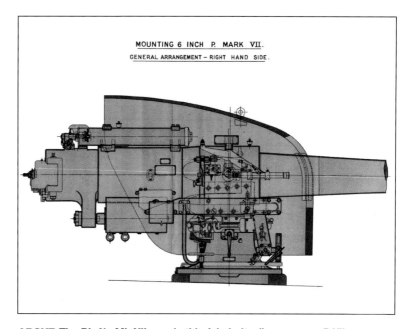

MOUNTING 6 INCH P. MARK VII.
GENERAL ARRANGEMENT – RIGHT HAND SIDE.

ABOVE The BL 6in Mk XII gun, in this Admiralty diagram on a P.VII mounting, was a common secondary armament on dreadnought battleships.

BELOW The Brazilian government also entered the dreadnought all-big-gun arms race with vessels such as the *Minas Geraes*, seen here boasting 12 × 12in guns.

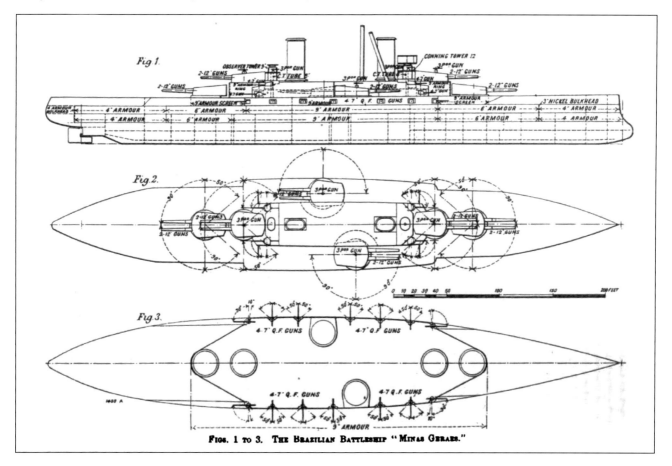

FIGS. 1 TO 3. THE BRAZILIAN BATTLESHIP "MINAS GERAES."

RIGHT A dramatic representation of *Dreadnought*'s searchlight piercing a gloomy northern sky.

BELOW This excellent photograph from the pre-dreadnought *Agamemnon* shows a 12-pdr gun in an anti-aircraft attitude, framed by a rangefinder operator to the left and a searchlight crew to the right.

searchlight itself, the following signals being made from the top of the fore chart-house:–

'Burn'	'Train right'
'Elevate'	'Train left'
'Depress'	'Sweep'

These orders being conveyed by electric lamps, which can be lit or extinguished by means of switches on top of the fore chart-house.

Report on Experimental Cruise, 1907

In 1903, development began in earnest to produce a new 4in high-velocity gun, to give a boost to British warship secondary armament. The output of this development entered service with the *Bellerophon* class of dreadnoughts as the 4in BL Mk VII and 4in guns would feature on dreadnoughts and super dreadnoughts until the 6in guns took over in the *Iron Duke* class. Set either on the deck or in hull sponsons, the guns measured 208.45in long and could throw out 4in shells at a muzzle velocity of 2,864ft/sec. The rate of fire was around 6–8rpm, and with an elevation of 15° the range was 11,600yd. Note that the maximum elevation of most of the mounts

BELOW An Ordnance BL 6in 45-calibre gun, on a P.IX mounting. This diagram shows details of the elevator and training gears.

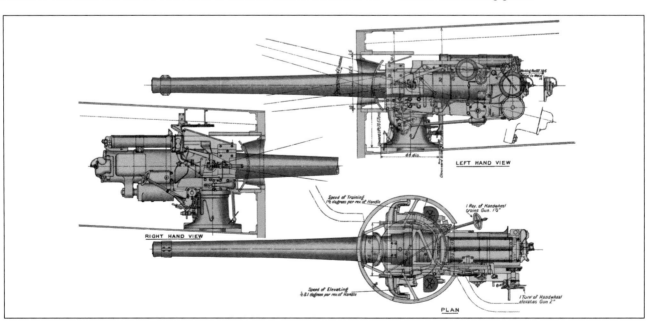

RIGHT The QF 12-pdr 18cwt guns on HMS *Dreadnought* could fire at a rate of 20rpm, and were primarily intended for anti-torpedo boat work.

CENTRE The combined weight of shot for a 12in gun broadside from *Dreadnought* was 6,800lb, depending on the shell type.

for the Mk VII (specifically the PII, PII*, PIV*, PIV**, PVI and PVIII) was 15°, but some guns were also set on HA (high-altitude) anti-aircraft mountings that had a maximum elevation of 60°. The guns were manually trained and fired by percussion or electrical ignition.

What the 6in guns offered was a far greater impact on target and a much-improved range capability, meaning that the battleship (or other vessel – the 6in guns were popular on a variety of ships) could engage torpedo boats at beyond-torpedo range. The Mk VII had a maximum range of 17,870yd at 20° elevation, although 15° was more typical of the full elevation of most of the mounts. Muzzle velocity from the 269.5in bore was 2,536ft/sec, while at 2,500yd the armour-piercing capped (APC) shells were capable of penetrating a single calibre of Krupp armour.

The downside of the 6in guns was that the heavy shells – each weighing around 100lb – resulted in slower rates of fire. Hoists were needed to supply the shells from the shell rooms, and during combat conditions it was recognised that these often couldn't keep the guns fed quickly enough to sustain their theoretical rate of fire of 5–7rpm. This rate could be achieved momentarily while the gunners were using up their ready ammunition, but once this was depleted the rate could drop down to just 3rpm.

The 6in gun type essentially questioned the all-big-gun philosophy, but it remained the preferred secondary armament for the rest of the super dreadnought types. Other guns that could be found aboard dreadnoughts and super dreadnoughts were small deck-mounted saluting and/or signalling guns, plus 3in anti-aircraft guns, to deal with the nascent threat from maritime air power.

LEFT The scale of 15in naval shells is apparent in this photograph. Shell weight was just under 2,000lb.

67
FIREPOWER

BELOW This cross-section diagram of a 15in naval shell illustrates the limited space for explosive filling plus the location of the base inertia fuse.

BELOW RIGHT A contemporary illustration of a bagged quarter-charge of Cordite MD, four of which could be used in a dreadnought 12in gun.

While the secondary armament on Britain's battleships typically had unitary shell and case designs, for the main guns the propellant and shells were stored and loaded as separate entities. The propellant favoured by the Royal Navy was known as Cordite MD, this being adopted at the turn of the 20th century as an improved version of the Cordite Mk I. Compared to its predecessor, the Cordite MD (composition: 65% guncotton, 30% nitroglycerine, 5% petroleum jelly) was more stable than Cordite Mk I, and actually required 15% more weight to deliver the same muzzle velocity. It was, however, far less corrosive than the Mk I formula, essentially doubling the life of the barrel. The cordite was stored in quarter-charge silk bags, packed in behind the shell according to the amount of power required. When the propellant was detonated, the bag was instantly burned away.

In terms of the shells used, by the dreadnought era armour penetration was imperative, so the most common shells for naval battle were armour-piercing varieties. The most basic of these was the standard armour-piercing (AP) shell, containing only 3–5% high-explosive filling, detonated by an inertia-activated fuse set in the base of the shell. With its forged steel, heat-hardened body, the AP shell was designed to penetrate deep into an enemy warship's structure before the rapid deceleration triggered the fuse. However, with increased depths and improved thicknesses of armour came the need for greater penetrative abilities. This gave rise to APC shells. With these shells, the nose was fitted with a steel cap that served to weaken the impact area before the hardened steel nose of the shell could effect its penetration. In contrast, however, there were also Semi-Armour-Piercing (SAP) warheads, which had deliberately reduced penetration so that they could be fired at (relatively) soft-skinned smaller warships, without the shell passing straight through before detonation.

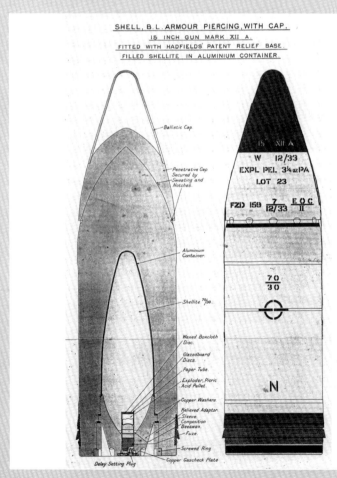

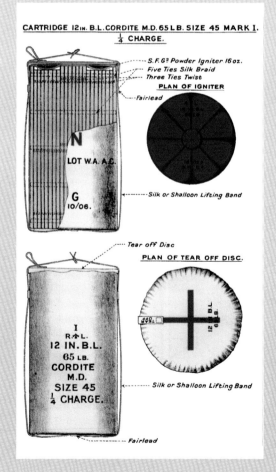

Torpedo tubes

The dreadnoughts and the super dreadnoughts carried two to four submerged torpedo tubes, initially of 18in diameter rising later to 21in. The pay-off for the investment in torpedo technology on these huge ships is questionable – they were fired very infrequently in battle, and in some cases spaces devoted to torpedo storage were eventually turned over to far more desirable magazines for HA ammunition. In his book *The Grand Fleet*, naval historian David K. Brown notes the problems associated with torpedo tubes and their ammunition spaces:

> The hazards of a torpedo armament were of two kinds, the first being the carriage of some 2–3 tons of high explosive, a risk increased in some wartime battlecruisers with above-water tubes. The second and more serious risk was of flooding in the large spaces needed to operate torpedoes. In Dreadnought the torpedo room was the full width of the hold and 24ft long with a door, low down, into the warhead room which was itself 24ft long. Later ships had even larger spaces. The flooding of Lutzow was due in considerable part to the big torpedo flat and leakage from it through a 'watertight' door. As with the 6in secondary battery, the torpedo armament of capital ships was expensive, ineffective and a potential hazard.

The torpedo tubes themselves were of a new Type B, which had a redesigned 'chopper' rear door that, when combined with the side door, made the side-loading of the torpedoes more convenient. It should be noted, however, that the ingress of water through the torpedo tubes during emergency loading could result in the torpedo-room operators sloshing around in several feet of water.

Fire control

Accurate, controllable and responsive fire control was one of the fundamental challenges of the era of the big gun. The computations that had to be fed into the gunlaying process were multiple and complex

– the range and bearing of the enemy, and its predicted manoeuvres before gun firing and during shell flight; the movement of the firing ship relative to the enemy ship; the pitch and roll of the ship in the sea; the arcing trajectory of the shell; the ballistic conditions prevailing; the condition of the gun and the type of ammunition used – the list went on.

Technical and tactical improvements in fire control – the method of delivering shells accurately on target – had been in development since the end of the 19th century. Aided by the more rapid training capabilities of hydraulically powered mounts, gunners began using a 'continuous aim' principle – actually keeping their guns on target throughout ship movement, rather than waiting with fixed barrels for a particular point in the roll to fire. This was a procedural improvement, but the real

ABOVE This photograph shows the Elswick 21in torpedo tube's side-loading arrangement, for fast and convenient loading.

BELOW An Italian battleship crew roll a 21in torpedo out ready for loading into the tube, visible on the left of the picture.

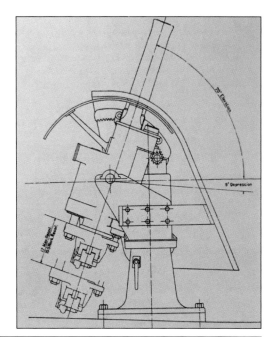

RIGHT A 4.7in naval gun showing its elevation and depression, plus the breech recoil distance.

BELOW An early Barr and Stroud rangefinder with a four-man crew. The operators would typically focus the rangefinder on a mast, funnel or other upright object with sharp lines.

empowerment of the long-range big gun came from technology.

First came the rangefinder, which emerged functionally in the 1890s. *Dreadnought* was fitted with two Barr and Stroud 9ft rangefinders, located on the foretop and a platform from the signal tower. Basically the rangefinder consisted of two lenses or mirrors separated by a fixed distance (9ft in the case of *Dreadnought*'s devices). Viewing an enemy ship produced a split image through the viewfinder, which could be used to calculate the ship's range through triangulation as the two parts of the image were adjusted to correspond. In British battleships, the 9ft rangefinders (including gyro-stabilised versions) were the standard until after the Battle of Jutland, when 15ft rangefinders were installed.

A more complex issue for those seeking accurate long-range gunnery was that of calculating the range rate and deflection, the rate at which the bearing and the distance of the enemy ship changed relative to the position of the firing ship. The rate of change was, especially in the fluid manoeuvres of combat, in a state of constant flux, so was hard to pin down. Yet the pioneering work of gunnery lieutenant John Saumarez Dumaresq resulted in a mechanical means of turning the estimated course and speed estimates into bearing models, presented on a 'table' that showed the range rate and deflection – information that could be transmitted to the gun crews. *Dreadnought* was pioneering in using a Vickers electrical transmitting system, which sent the gunnery information down to the

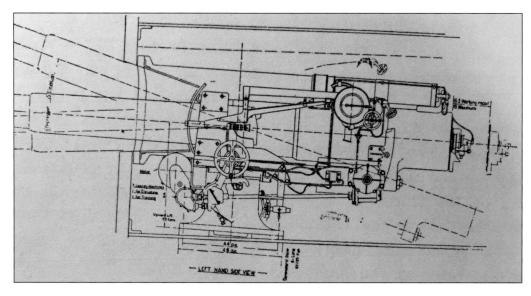

RIGHT A Vickers 6in 50-calibre gun, with electrical elevating and training gear.

guns, presenting it mechanically on a pointer dial that indicated the range and deflection. *Dreadnought* also featured two transmitting stations – one in the lower conning tower and one in the lower signal tower – with all the turrets wired to each of the transmitting stations, to ensure that gun direction could continue if one of the stations was put out of action.

A useful description of the relationship between guns and a transmitting station comes from a pre-war Royal Navy gunnery report. Here it does not relate to the *Dreadnought*'s main gun armament, but to its secondary armament. Nevertheless, the principles of interaction between the transmitting station and the guns are applicable more generally:

The guns are in 12 groups of two guns each, six groups on each side of the ship, the three forward gun groups on each side controlled from main control position (on the big tripod mast), and the three after gun groups on each side controlled from the top of the after signal tower. Each group of guns is limited to an arc of training of 30°.

The six forward guns are controlled from main control position as follows:–

Range and deflection are called down voice-pipe to main transmitting station (fore lower conning tower) whence it is sent to the gun group by Vickers range and deflection transmitters. The order 'First' is called down the voice-pipe to the main transmitting station, when it is sent to the gun group by the fire-gong. There is no means of giving any orders to the guns except by the fire-gong and the check fire disc.

The six after gun groups are controlled from the top of the after signal tower through the lower signal tower in exactly the same way as the forward gun groups are through the main transmitted station. A plate is fitted to each 12-pr. mounting to carry a Vickers combined range and deflection receiver and a fire-gong.

There were other devices used by the dreadnoughts and super dreadnoughts to enhance accuracy. For example, from 1906 the Royal Navy relied upon the Vickers Clock, a spinning-wheel device that calculated future

ABOVE The transmitting station of HMS *Belfast*, including a fire-control table, gives a good general impression of what such a station might look like in a dreadnought-era battleship. *(Rémi Kaupp)*

range of the target ship based on the current range and range rate. Improved versions from other manufacturers appeared, most prominently the Argo Clock from 1912.

The combination of accurate rangefinders and rate of change tables, plus automatic transmission of the data to the guns, revolutionised battleship firepower and accuracy, although visual spotting and verbal adjustment remained key elements of the fire-control process. Each nation in the

BELOW This illustration from the *Gunnery Pocket Book* provides a diagrammatic explanation of the layout of a fire-control table.

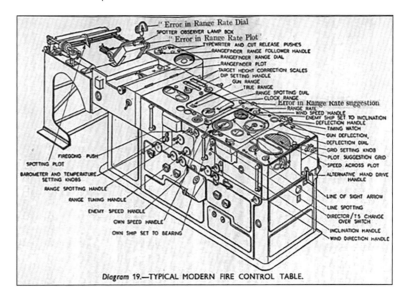

Diagram 19.—TYPICAL MODERN FIRE CONTROL TABLE.

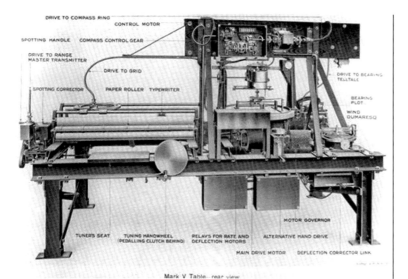

ABOVE The Mk V Dreyer Fire-Control Table, as fitted aboard the battlecruiser HMS *Hood*, was the culmination of the Dreyer Fire Table installed in battleships from 1911.

dreadnought/super dreadnought race developed its own similar technologies.

Two more seminal steps in dreadnought fire control need to be explained. The first of these was the Dreyer Fire Table, invented in 1911 and improved frequently thereafter. The Dreyer Fire Table was literally a large table, to which and in which were mounted a plethora of electromechanical fire computation devices, some of which have been mentioned previously. Each of the devices was interconnected to rationalise the varieties of inputted information into a single fire solution. If we look at the Mk III Fire Table, which was introduced in about 1918, the information streaming into the device included:

- Range rates
- Target range estimates
- Target heading/speed estimates

RIGHT Another view of 'Togo', the ship's cat, this time seen with the muzzle itself of *Dreadnought*'s 12in guns. Note how the muzzle shows the multi-tube construction of the gun. (NMRN)

- Observed target relative bearing
- Own ship heading
- Own ship speed
- Spotting corrections
- Apparent wind speed
- Apparent wind direction
- Adjustments to range.

This information flowed in from various locations and personnel around the ship, and was then processed into gun output data by a variety of the manual and automatic processes. Once the calculations had taken place, the gunhouse crews would then receive the following information:

- Gun range
- Range rate
- Gun deflection
- Enemy speed
- Enemy inclination to line of bearing.

In essence, the Fire Table was a large analogue fire-control computer, and although its performance was variable at times – it depended heavily on high-quality information inputted and timely processing of that information – it was certainly a profitable addition to the fire control of the big-gun battleships.

One issue that had to be addressed with the emergence of *Dreadnought* was that of gun synchronisation. It was all very well having individual gun turrets blasting away at the target, but for maximum effect and controllability it was better to have some or all of the turrets synchronised in their fire, both in terms of the moment of firing and of the point of aim. The Navy's *Gunnery Pocket Book* of 1945, although slightly beyond our focal period (the 1945 version was actually an update of the original 1932 edition), neatly explained the problems of non-synchronised fire:

(i) *It is difficult to point out a target to several gunlayers simultaneously.*
(ii) *The guns, being comparatively low down near the water-line, do not get a very good view of distant targets.*
(iii) *Being low down near the water-line the telescopes of the gun-sights are liable to be clouded by spray.*

(iv) Each gunlayer has his own individual error, and though these errors may be small, they accumulate and cause the shots of a salvo to fall some considerable distance apart from each other.

(v) It is most unlikely that all the gunlayers in the ship will fire at the same instant; as a result there may be an appreciable period during which one or more guns will be firing and making noise and smoke.

(vi) As all the guns are more or less on the same level, the smoke from some guns is bound to cause interference in the laying of other guns.

(vii) Spotting the fall of shot from a number of guns fired one after the other is extremely difficult.

Gunnery Pocket Book, 1945

To achieve synchronisation, however, posed several levels of challenge. First, the length of the ship meant that to aim at a common point each gun barrel couldn't be set parallel to one another, but had to have a point of convergence. Second, someone had to be able to control and initiate the coordinated fire at an instant – verbal or other auditory signals would still likely produce a staggered pattern of fire. Third, whoever was responsible for the fire had to have some method of transmitting fire data to the guns, in coordination with the information from other fire-control technologies.

The solution was the 'director' system. Essentially, the director was a device, looking much like a theodolite, which was set in the ship's tops, and which acted like a coordinating gunsight for the battery of guns. Operated by a director team of about 3–4 men, the director received information from the transmitting station to which it added elevation and training angle information, which could be sent directly to the gun crews to apply the adjustments. This meant that the gun crews themselves were now no longer in control of the training and elevation. The director officer could also fire the guns himself through an electrical trigger system mounted in the director position.

The first of the dreadnoughts to take director fire was HMS *Bellerophon*, but thereafter directors became standard fitting on British battleships. Although director fire was far from perfect, and

ABOVE The 15in guns in their superfiring turrets aboard HMS *Queen Elizabeth*. The maximum range of these guns was more than 33,000yd.

also generally served to slow down the rate of fire, it certainly enhanced the concentration of fire.

The big-gun debate

We have already charted something of the course of the armament debate that led to, and surrounded, the dreadnought battleships. The arguments for the all-big-gun warship were controversial, and remain so among those for whom naval warfare is an intellectual passion. Advocates for the new layout argued that the emphasis on big guns meant that engagements would be decided before enemy vessels could close to short range, and with shells that would have a decisive effect on the structures of heavily armoured capital ships. The detractors countered with assertions that rapid fire from substantial secondary guns would provide destructive

BELOW A gunner is dragged through the bore of a 12in gun; sometimes this was done to facilitate the cleaning of the rifling.

RIGHT Gunners carefully use a mechanical hoist to winch 13.5in shells aboard a super dreadnought battleship, before transferring them down to the shell rooms.

saturation of a target that the big guns would struggle to match.

The full intricacies of this argument are explored in exhaustive detail in other volumes. By way of illustration, however, we do well to examine a dreadnought defence from a 'Paper Prepared by the Director of Naval Ordnance – *Considerations of the Design of a Battleship*'. What is particularly interesting about this account – part of which is reproduced here – is that the author takes on the esteemed American naval strategist Alfred Thayer Mahan, author of the landmark work *The Influence of Sea Power Upon History, 1660–1783* (1890). In the following passage, the author centrally addresses the comparison of the big guns with smaller calibres:

> *It is undoubtedly true that guns of 10-inch, 9.2-inch, or 6-inch calibre will, owing to their greater rapidity of fire and the larger number that can be carried for the same weight, obtain a greater number of hits than 12-inch guns in a given time at all probable fighting range, but the increased rate of hitting with the smaller gun will be in any way proportionate to its maximum possible rate of fire as compared to that of the larger gun. Because for instance a 6-inch gun at gunlayers' test has made 11 hits in one minute it is entirely erroneous to deduce, as some writers would argue, that a broadside of five 6-inch guns would plant 55 hits per minute on an enemy. Recent experience, which is very considerable, shows that the technical requirements for attaining the highest accuracy of shooting at all ranges under battle conditions preclude entirely the effective use of more than*

a certain number of guns of the calibres under consideration or more than a certain rate of fire. 12-inch, 10-inch, and 9.2-inch and less calibres all come under precisely the same conditions in this respect. Therefore the inherent possibility of obtaining largely increased numbers and a much greater rate of fire from the lesser calibres cannot be realised in practice.

This disposes of the argument put forward even by so skilled a writer as Captain Mahan in the May number of the 'National Review', where he states:–

'Tactically a fleet of "Dreadnoughts," in action with the type hitherto in favour, requires distant firing. It therefore has received a check when an opponent can advance numerous lighter guns within effective range of its fewer heavier, which will reproduce in great measure the fight of a fleet with an embrasured fort, where large superiority in number of guns, and nearness, were essential factors to success, by beating down the personnel under a storm of light missiles, such as grape and canister. In such cases, volume of fire was relied upon to counterbalance, offensively, the great defensive inferiority of the ships' sides; and in the case of ship against ship, where so great defensive disparity will not obtain, it is well within the limits of probability that a great volume of fire may prove distinctly superior to one of less diffusion, although of equal weight.'

It is improbable that Captain Mahan has ever seen fleet firing under modern conditions or he would hardly have fallen into such error as the quotation above shows, and he would realise that the ship armed with a lighter nature of gun would be disabled long before she could close sufficiently to use them with effect even assuming her to have the advantage of speed.

> *Considerations of the Design of a Battleship*, pp. 18–19

Although not all battle-tested authorities come to the same conclusion as in the passage above, the author does make the important distinction between theory and experience. The author argues that in the new era of the big guns, ships with lesser calibres predominating are at an automatic disadvantage, a disadvantage that would soon be exposed once 12in shells began to roar in, and at

extreme ranges. Although this chapter has focused largely on a technical and structural description of dreadnought gunnery, we do need to remind ourselves of the psychological and physical impact of the new big-gun battleships. A full broadside of 12in firepower, landing in close proximity to the enemy ship or ploughing directly into its masts, decks or other structures, must have left an impression as awe-inspiring as it was appalling. Against such firepower, any theoretical argument could be fundamentally weakened.

GUNNERY REPORT ON EXPERIMENTAL CRUISE

The gunnery practices were of two distinct natures:–
1) Heavy gun firing to test the best method of firing the guns so as to obtain the greatest rapidity and freedom from 'smoke interference,' and also to determine the best form of control both when firing at a single ship, and also with one broadside at two ships.
2) The best grouping and control of the light Q.F. armament to repel torpedo craft by day and by night.

The details of the firings will be found in various appendices and reports attached to the gunnery and searchlight sections.

Briefly, the more important conclusions arrived at were as follows:–
1) Smoke difficulties with three-quarter charges in this climate were found to be slight. I hope to be allowed to repeat some of the firing with full charges under the climatic conditions of the English Channel, but I do not anticipate that even there any great difficulties will be found to exist.
2) The control of the guns was found to be simple, both from aloft, and from the control position on top of the signal tower.
3) The shooting gave promise and very efficient firing in action, both as regards rapidity and accuracy.
4) The type of armament was far simpler and more accurate to control than a mixed armament.

As regards the light Q.F. firing, the methods adopted were primarily governed by the consideration that the system of control must be such as could be carried out on the night following a day action, and after the ship had been submitted to shell-fire.

I have no believer [*sic*] in attempting to forecast the probable success or a torpedo attack in war time from the results of firing at a canvas target at night, or by attacking ships with destroyers when only blank ammunition is fired;

but night firing, if rigidly carried out, affords an excellent opportunity of judging the progress made in the defence of ships against torpedo attack.

The conclusions arrived at were:–
1) The result of the night firing was satisfactory, showing that five or six hits would probably be made by four guns on a target the size of a destroyer, or on each of the two targets the size of the destroyer, between the ranges of 2,500 and 1,500 yards.
2) The results are capable of great improvement in the near future, since many weak points in our methods and practice were brought to light during the firing. I am bound to admit that this is the only night firing I have ever witnessed which in any way has led me to hope that a ship might be defended by gun-fire against a torpedo attack at night.
3) Ranging salvoes then breaking into independent firing appears to be the most satisfactory system.
4) The telaupad system of control is far and away the most efficient.
5) The control of the guns should be aloft.
6) The control of the lights should be near the captain.
7) These two controls should therefore be dissociated.
8) The arcs of training of both guns and searchlights should be unlimited.
9) Better vent-sealing tubes are required in high-pressure guns.
10) A 24-in. projector is practically as good as a 36-in.
11) The relative efficiency of two 24-in. projectors compared with one 36-in. requires further trial.

R.C. Bacon, *Report on the Experimental Cruise*, 1907, p. 5

Chapter Four

Propulsion and electrical systems

The dreadnoughts and super dreadnoughts were the most powerful ships on the seas during the first half of the 20th century. They delivered a performance that combined speed with the manoeuvrability necessary for rapid tactical positioning.

OPPOSITE Giving some impression of the sheer scale of battleship propulsion, here are the triple screws of the Russian battleship *Poltava*.

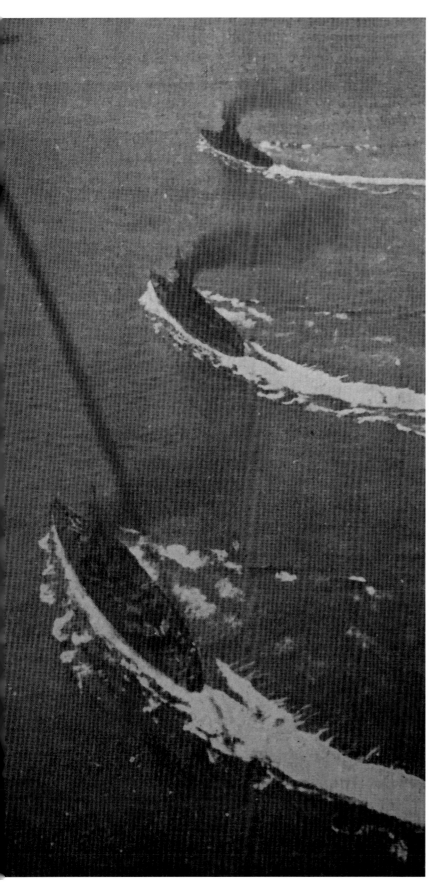

LEFT British capital warships perform a simultaneous manoeuvre. It would take about 12–15 seconds to turn a large battleship over to helm.

A ship of any significant size is a mechanically complex creation. The engineering and design process has to take into account fitments that range from the powerplant at the heart of the ship, through to minor electrical switches for lights and ducts for ventilation. Any deficiencies in this overall design, especially in the way all the components integrate with one another, reveal themselves in sharp silhouettes once a ship begins its operational life.

In this chapter, we focus our attention principally on the powerplant and electrical systems of *Dreadnought* specifically. We examine this ship in detail mainly because it is the foundation of all the other dreadnoughts and super dreadnoughts that followed, but also because any attempt to review the mechanical arrangements of all the battleships would be vast in scope. The bibliography to this book lists several works that enable the reader to explore other warships in more depth, but *Dreadnought* remains a good yardstick by which to measure warship design in general during the period in question.

Turbine power

The dreadnoughts and super dreadnoughts were mechanically powerful ships – of that there can be no doubt. By way of comparison, many modern destroyers average around 500ft in length, have a displacement of some 8,000 tons and, typically powered by an array of gas turbines, can make speeds of around 30 knots quite comfortably. Back in 1915, the British launched HMS *Royal Sovereign*, which measured 624ft and had a fully laden displacement of 31,000 tons. Nevertheless, such a hulking ship could still make 23 knots, driven by its Parsons steam turbines and fuelled by boilers that generated 40,000shp. Such figures remain respectable even more than 100 years later.

The Parsons name is a good hook on which to hang our initial discussion of the dreadnought powerplants, as it was a name that dominated

DREADNOUGHT BATTLESHIP MANUAL

British naval propulsion for crucial decades in its history. Charles Parsons was a British engineer who, during the 1880s, began experimenting with turbine powerplant systems in marine contexts, as replacements for reciprocating engines. In summary, turbines work by delivering the thermal energy of pressurised steam to blades on a rotary shaft, the steam pressure turning the shaft to provide rotary output power. Parsons built upon previous early work in turbine technology, and sought to improve the efficiency of the engine type. How

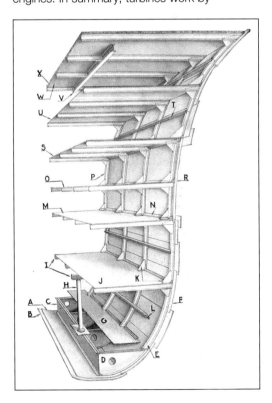

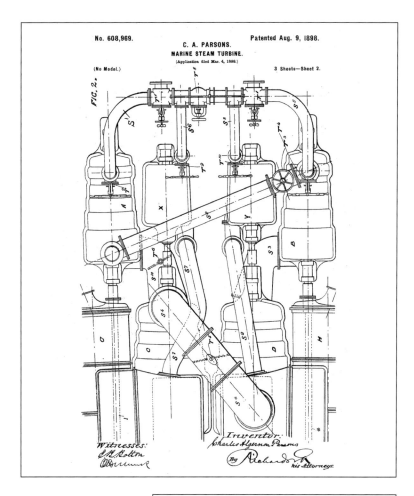

No. 608,969.

C. A. PARSONS.
MARINE STEAM TURBINE.
(Application filed Mar. 4, 1898.)

Patented Aug. 9, 1898.

(No Model.)

3 Sheets—Sheet 2.

FIG. 2.

Witnesses:
Inventor:
Charles Algernon Parsons
By Richardson
his Attorneys.

he did so is explained in a lecture paper he wrote in about 1904:

In 1884 or four years previously, I dealt with the turbine problem in a different way. It seemed to me that moderate surface velocities and speeds of rotation were essential if the turbine motor was to receive general acceptance as a prime mover. I therefore decided to split up the fall in pressure of the steam into small fractional expansions over a large number of turbines in series, so that the velocity of the steam nowhere should be great. Consequently, as we shall see later, a moderate speed of turbine suffices for the highest economy. This principle of compounding turbines in series is now universally used in all except very small engines, where economy in steam is of secondary importance. The arrangement of small falls in pressure at each turbine also appeared to me to be surer to give a high efficiency, because the steam flowed practically in a non-expansive manner through each individual turbine, and consequently in an analogous way to water in hydraulic turbines whose high

ABOVE AND RIGHT
These diagrams are from Parsons's patent application of 1898 for his steam turbines. The Parsons steam turbine would be the heart of almost all the dreadnought and super dreadnought battleships.

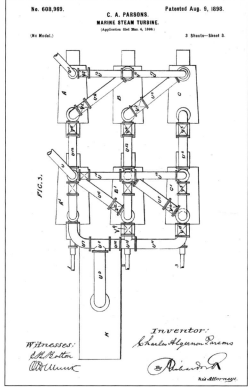

No. 608,969.

C. A. PARSONS.
MARINE STEAM TURBINE.
(Application filed Mar. 4, 1898.)

Patented Aug. 9, 1898.

(No Model.)

3 Sheets—Sheet 3.

FIG. 3.

Witnesses:
Inventor:
Charles Algernon Parsons
By Richardson
his Attorneys.

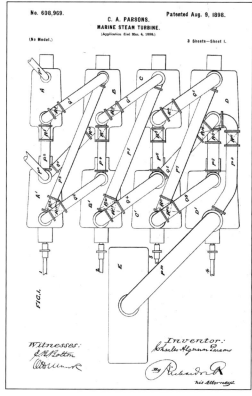

No. 608,969.

C. A. PARSONS.
MARINE STEAM TURBINE.
(Application filed Mar. 4, 1898.)

Patented Aug. 9, 1898.

(No Model.)

3 Sheets—Sheet 1.

FIG. 1.

Witnesses:
Inventor:
Charles Algernon Parsons
By Richardson
his Attorneys.

efficiency at that date had been proved by accurate tests.

Parsons, 'The Steam Turbine', c1904

Parsons was soon proving the success of his design. The first turbine-powered ship in history, the *Turbinia*, was launched in 1894 and was given motion by a three-stage axial-flow direct-acting (i.e. not geared) Parsons steam turbine, which made the 104ft craft for a time the fastest ship on the waves, although the ship did experience some issues with cavitation (explained and discussed below). Further military commissions followed, with Parsons turbines fitted to two Navy destroyers – HMS *Viper* and HMS *Cobra* – at the turn of the 20th century. Parsons's momentum was building, and it was in 1906 that three great ships took to the waves all powered by Parsons turbines – the legendary civil liners *Lusitania* and *Mauretania*, and the battleship *Dreadnought*.

Dreadnought's powerplant

At the heart of *Dreadnought* were installed two sets of Parsons turbines, each driving two shafts. The arrangement of the turbines mirrored each other in near-identical engine rooms. The two outer turbines of the configuration were high-pressure (HP) types, while those on the inner shafts were low-pressure (LP) versions, these also being fitted with cruising turbines to improve the performance at slower speeds. Each HP shaft was fitted with one HP ahead and one HP astern, and each inner shaft also had LP ahead and astern. Total designed shaft horsepower was 23,000, and all the shafts had a designed speed of 320rpm.

This was the *Dreadnought* as it was originally configured and went into service. One significant early change was that maintenance in the winter of 1907 revealed that the 6,000shp cruising turbines had developed significant problems.

John Roberts's book, *The Battleship Dreadnought*, explains the reason behind these problems, in that the time the cruising turbines spent idling resulted in drag on the shafts and subsequent difficulties in controlling turbine temperature. These issues had a detrimental

effect on the metallurgical integrity of the turbine blades; the 1907 investigation revealed that many blades in the 2nd and 3rd expansion stages had been stripped off, and that there were cracked casings. For this reason, the cruising turbines were eventually disconnected and remained aboard the ship, albeit non-functional, for the rest of her career.

ABOVE AND BELOW LEFT Construction of the turbines for HMS *Bellerophon* at the Fairfield Shipbuilding and Engineering Company in Govan, Scotland.

The Parsons turbines, while having some limitations at certain points of the power spectrum, were generally excellent performers. This much became evident from the Experimental Cruise, as is explained by one R.C. Bacon in his *Report on the Experimental Cruise*:

The turbines have worked perfectly. The ship has steamed 11,000 miles. I'm practically requiring no readjustment of bearings. Had the engines been of the reciprocating type there can be no doubt but that constant readjustment of bearings would have been necessary. To steam from Gibraltar to Trinidad, 3,500 miles, at 17 knots, and to arrive there with nothing requiring to be done to the main engines of any sort, is sufficient criticism of this class of machinery. It must not be forgotten that the realisation of these results with a new type of gear speaks well for the care and energy of Engineer Commander Onyon and his staff. In other respects besides reliability the engines have been satisfactory, since they manoeuvre quickly and with certainty. The ventilation of the engine rooms is dealt with later. The auxiliary engines have, with the exception of

the steering engines (previously reported on) been satisfactory.

R.C. Bacon, *Report on the Experimental Cruise*, 1907, p. 4

The power for *Dreadnought*'s turbines came from a total of 18 Babcock and Wilcox water-tube boilers, arranged in groups of six in three boiler spaces. In its most basic description, a water-tube boiler works by heating water to boiling point and beyond as it passes through a space heated from a furnace. The pressurised steam produced in the process is then drawn off into a steam drum, then (for turbine engines) channelled back through the heating process to become a dry, superheated gas that can then be directed against the turbine blades.

The Babcock and Wilcox boilers had a normal working pressure of 250psi, which dropped down to 185psi at the face of the turbine blades. An article from the *Journal of the American Society for Naval Engineers* described the boilers in some more detail in its 1906 article, 'Trials of H.M.S. *Dreadnought*':

She [Dreadnought] has eighteen Babcock & Wilcox boilers, each of twenty elements,

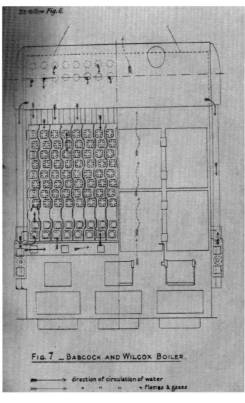

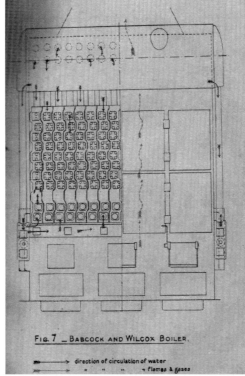

RIGHT Two diagrams explaining the function of the Babcock and Wilcox boiler, taken from the *Stoker's Manual* of 1912.

FIG. 7 _ BABCOCK AND WILCOX BOILER.

→ direction of circulation of water
" " " " → Flames & gases

FIG. 8 _ BABCOCK AND WILCOX BOILER.

→ direction of circulation of water
" " " " → Flames & gases.

arranged in three stokeholds, and fitted for burning oil fuel in conjunction with coal. The grate surface is 1,560 square feet, the heating surface 55,400 square feet, and the tops of her funnels are about 85 feet above the fire-bars. Each stokehold has a tube, about 30 inches in diameter, which can be used for raising ashes, or wounded, by electric lifts. See's ash ejectors are also fitted. Each stokehold is self-contained. The main condensors [sic] have 26,000 square feet of cooling surface, the auxiliary condensors 6,000'.

Some points of this description are worth expansion. As noted, *Dreadnought* was capable of running on both oil and coal. The onboard coal storage, at normal capacity, was 900 tons, going up to a maximum of 2,900 tons; total oil storage was 1,120 tons. One interesting aside about the coal-to-oil switch was that the coal storage compartments actually formed part of the anti-torpedo protection of many warships, the coal bunkers providing a space and a material filling that could to some degree 'soak up' the effects of a heavy hull explosion. Oil, being of limited compressibility and also being readily flammable, presented more of a risk to the ship, but ultimately was a risk worth accepting. With the addition of the oil fuel, *Dreadnought* had an operational radius of 6,620nm at 10 knots, but 4,340nm at the same speed relying on coal alone. At a power output of 2,220shp, the ship would eat its way through 127 tons of coal every 24 hours.

The *Journal of the American Society for Naval Engineers* article also makes note of ash ejectors, a critical mechanical feature in any coal-powered ship. Each boiler room had its own ash ejector, which consisted of a discharge pipe rising up from the stokehold to an ejection port set up the side of the hull. The ashes were pushed into a hopper that fed them through a grate into the discharge pipe, and the ashes were ejected by a blast of water at 200lb/sq in pressure from the boiler rooms' fire and bilge pumps. An alternative method was an ash hoist (actually little more than a bucket lift) for carrying loose ash up to the upper deck, but this was largely an emergency measure only, for

it resulted in polluting ash blowing around the deck areas. Note that with the introduction of purely oil-fired ships, out went the associated need for ash ejectors.

Dreadnought had many other pump systems fitted, including four 75-ton fire and bilge pumps in the engine rooms. There were also electric pumps placed in the watertight compartments, these able to pump out 50 tons of water each hour should the crew need to evacuate a flooded compartment with haste.

Regarding the coal bunkers, these were filled via fixed coaling chutes that ran between the upper and main decks. This configuration was an improvement over earlier practices, in which coal was transferred via canvas chutes, a process that usually ended up with a filthy ship. The coal bunkers were set amidships, with each boiler having its own set of dedicated bunkers. To ensure a watertight separation between the

ABOVE A diagram showing the arrangement of a dreadnought boiler room, plus the flow of steam, ingress of ventilation and the coaling supply.

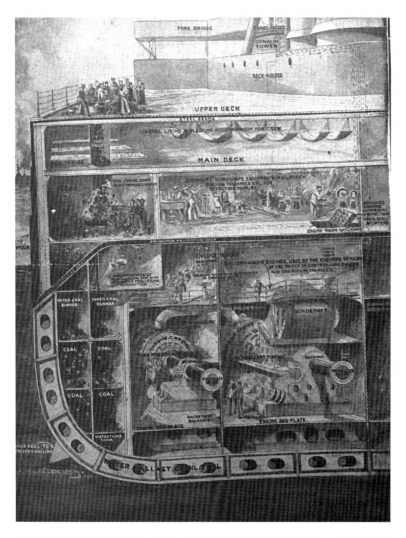

LEFT In this diagram we see the arrangement of the high-pressure and low-pressure turbines, plus the engineering spaces around the powerplants.

bunker and the boiler, the bulkheads were solid with no penetration by communication systems, although some of the bunkers had watertight doors fitted.

R.C. Bacon's *Report on the Experimental Cruise* (1907) raised a few issues about boiler construction, three of the most important given here:

1. *Bearer bars are somewhat light, and ½ in. thick, and distort easily, as also does the fore and aft girder on which the bearer bar rests. This is very thin indeed.*
2. *All cast iron in furnaces should be protected by brick or clay. The furnace frames or mouthpieces should be given sufficient room for expansion, so as to prevent fouling the protection plates when hot, which causes the frames to distort and consequently jambs [sic] the furnace doors. The castings at the back of protection plates should be stronger and have clearance holes drilled to jig to suit spare protection plates and so avoid much fitting of studs to holes in lugs.*
3. *The boilers require larger running down valves to save time. This would also mean larger connections of reserve fresh-water tanks.*

Before looking at other aspects of *Dreadnought*'s engineering arrangements, we should note the steady increase in turbine power across the dreadnoughts and super dreadnoughts which took place as the technology was refined and improved. Hence while *Dreadnought* generated 23,000shp, the *Royal Sovereign* class nearly doubled that figure, to 40,000shp.

LEFT A Babcock and Wilcox boiler. The furnace would be built beneath the bank of water tubes, and the large tank at the top is the steam and water drum. The U-bend pipe in the middle is the superheater.

MAIN POWER ARRANGEMENTS OF THE DREADNOUGHTS AND SUPER DREADNOUGHTS

Ship/Class	Powerplant	Boilers	Shp
Dreadnought	Parsons direct-drive turbines driving four propellers	18 × Babcock and Wilcox	23,000
Bellerophon	Parsons direct-drive turbines driving four propellers	18 × Babcock and Wilcox (Yarrow in *Temeraire*)	23,000
St Vincent	Parsons direct-drive turbines driving four propellers	18 × Babcock and Wilcox (Yarrow in *Collingwood*)	24,500
Neptune	Parsons direct-drive turbines driving four propellers	18 × Yarrow	25,000
Colossus	Parsons direct-drive turbines driving four propellers	18 × Babcock and Wilcox (Yarrow in *Hercules*)	25,000
Agincourt	Parsons direct-drive turbines driving four propellers	22 × Babcock and Wilcox	34,000
Orion	Parsons direct-drive turbines driving four propellers	18 × Yarrow (Babcock and Wilcox in *Monarch*)	27,000
King George V	Parsons direct-drive turbines driving four propellers	18 × Babcock and Wilcox (Yarrow in *Audacious* and *Centurion*)	31,000
Iron Duke	Parsons direct-drive turbines driving four propellers	18 × Yarrow (Babcock and Wilcox in *Iron Duke* and *Benbow*)	29,000
Queen Elizabeth	Parsons reaction turbines driving four propellers	24 × Babcock and Wilcox	56,000
Royal Sovereign	Parsons reaction turbines driving four propellers	18 × Babcock and Wilcox (Yarrow in *Resolution* and *Royal Oak*)	40,000
Erin	Parsons direct-drive turbines driving four propellers	15 × Babcock and Wilcox	26,500
Canada	Parsons and Brown Curtis turbines driving four propellers	21 × Yarrow	37,000

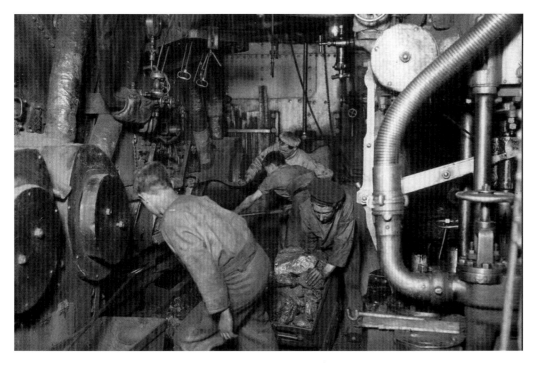

LEFT This image of life in the boiler room of *Royal Oak* gives an unequivocal impression of the hard physical labour involved in keeping the engines running.

85

Propellers and steering gear

The shafts from the turbines terminated in the ship's mighty three-bladed propellers, each (at the original point of design) 8ft 10in in diameter and with a blade area of 33sq ft. In May–June 1907, these were all replaced, with those on the inner shafts having a reduced area of 28sq ft and the outer shaft propellers having an increased area of 40sq ft.

A key challenge of steam turbine design was that of striking the right relationship between the speed of the turbine blades, and therefore of the rotor shaft, and that of the propeller in the water. Put simply, turbines worked at their greatest efficiency at high speeds, whereas propellers required turning at lower speeds to ensure that they delivered their force with optimal 'bite' on the water. This issue was addressed in dreadnought battleships through the use of a speed-reduction gear, explained here in *The Naval Annual 1913*:

The advantage which may accrue from the introduction of speed-reduction gear between the turbine and the propeller is easily explained. Popularly expressed, the thermodynamic efficiency of a turbine depends largely on this speed of the blades around the circumference of its rotor being in proper relation to the velocity of the steam impinging on the blades. The peripheral speed of the drum of a turbine carrying the blades therefore requires to be high. The screw propeller of a ship, after it exceeds a given rate of speed, falls off somewhat in efficiency owing to cavitation which, popularly explained, means the introduction of air in front of the blade surface. The result is not only a reduction in efficiency but serious deterioration of the metal by erosion. It is true that this latter difficulty has been partly overcome, but it is inevitable that with cavitation there should be great loss in the driving power of the screw. To overcome the difficulty a compromise was made by increasing the diameter of the turbine drum, so that the number of revolutions was reduced without a proportionate lessening of the blade speed, which could thus be kept not too much below the velocity of steam. At the same time the revolutions of the propeller were lessened. Increase in the diameter of the turbine rotor, however, involved considerable augmentation of weight. The difference in weight per H.P. of battleship and destroyer turbines is partly due to the latter being run at a greater number of revolutions per minute.

The Naval Annual 1913, p. 100

BELOW The stern of HMS *Dreadnought*, waiting for the fitting of her twin rudders plus the armour plating on the hull. (NMRN)

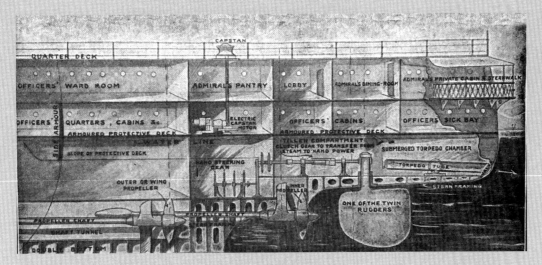

ADMIRALTY REPORT: 'SUGGESTED ALTERATIONS IN SHIPS OF DREADNOUGHT CLASS'

1 Efficient communication between the two starting platforms is essential. A 4-in. voice-pipe should be fitted above main deck between the engine-rooms at the manoeuvring valves, and a loud single-stroke gong in lieu of the present telephonic communication. This pipe can be led above the main deck, and the thwartship bulkhead between the engine rooms kept watertight.

3 The position of the distiller test tanks should be altered, and a stowage found inside the engine-room hatches to enable the tanks to be more easily under observation, and for the better preservation of the gauge-glasses and guards. At present they are placed immediately in the gangway of two ladders from the upper to main deck.

4 Complete jointless lengths of steam-pipes should be fitted in spaces between the main machinery and boiler compartments, as great difficulty has been experienced in making awkward joints in these confined spaces.

6 Arrangements for escape of air from reserve feed and oil-tanks should be made more efficient by cutting more holes in longitudinals, as at present water and oil will not level off for some hours, and filling has to take place very slowly. This is important, as a list to the ship materially increases her draft [sic].

7 Generally it would be better not to attach oil-boxers to steam cylinders, but to fit them to bulkheads adjacent, as the oil gets very thin and hot. The dripping could be more easily regulated and the oil would remain cooler.

11 Spring-loaded valves for escape of excess exhaust steam to auxiliary condenser should be placed in a more accessible position, since, at present, a proper adjustment of these valves is very hard to carry out.

14 A complete range of auxiliary steam pipe should be carried right around the engine and boiler rooms. The disposition of the coal is such that the forward group of boilers should be used as little as possible in harbour. With either of the other groups of boilers in use the auxiliary steam pipe forward of them has usually to be kept under steam, and the fact of there being little or no circulation of steam through this end of the pipe causes water to accumulate which finds its way out through joints and expansion glands.

17 The ice machine and refrigerator engine should both be fitted with weeds traps and also the ice machine with a non-return valve close to the sea inlet, as both these engines have been frequently choked with jelly fish, and the process of clearing occupies considerable time. The ice machine be situated on the upper deck, considerable difficulties experienced on starting machine in getting the circulating pump to heave.

24 The crush shaft between the two steering engines should be made in three pieces instead of two. There should be a flanged coupling in the port engine-room as well as in the starboard, and a short middle piece of shaft, some 6 feet in length. The present long piece cannot be removed clear of the steering engine. The plummer block for port centre shaft and the steering engine cross shaft being removed.

R.C. Bacon, *Report on the Experimental Cruise*, Section II, 'Suggested Alterations in Ships of "Dreadnought" Class', 1907.

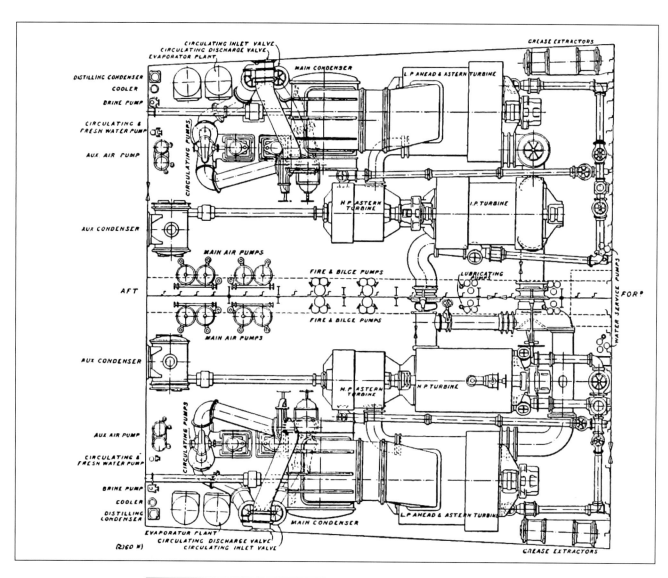

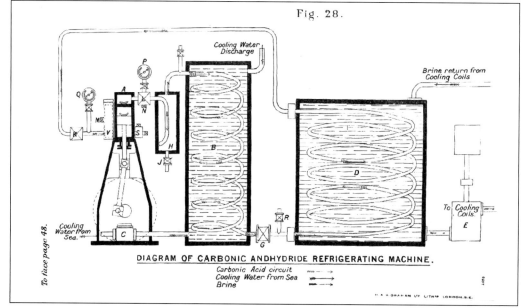

ABOVE A diagram from a 1911 lecture on warship propulsion, showing turbine arrangement for a four-screw battleship.

RIGHT Another image from *The Stoker's Manual* of 1912, this time explaining the principles of on-board refrigeration, which was crucial to ensuring the longevity of food supplies.

Fig. 28.

DIAGRAM OF CARBONIC ANDHYDRIDE REFRIGERATING MACHINE.

Carbonic Acid circuit
Cooling Water from Sea
Brine

RIGHT Yarrow boilers were, alongside those from Babcock and Wilcox, the beating heart of many of the world's warships. These are destined for a Chilean dreadnought, c1912.

With the problems of cavitation solved, the dreadnought and super dreadnought battleships could perform with control and dexterity at lower speeds, as attested to by numerous reports from the era. Of course, the ship also had to be steered, and direction was delivered through twin underhung rudders in the transverse section. (A single rudder would have given the ship an unacceptably large turning circle.) Two sets of control shafting were fitted within the ship, one set to port and one to starboard, the shafting running down to the steering engines that powered the rudders. Note, however, that each control shaft was linked to both steering engines, although a clutch system meant that only one shaft could operate a steering engine at any one time. The doubling-up was a complicated but sensible arrangement. It meant that if one control shaft was damaged by, say, a torpedo strike, the ship could still be steered via the other shaft. In the case of a dire emergency, should the standard mechanical control system break down entirely, the ship also included a manual steering compartment at the very back of the ship, in which manual brute force could be used to keep the vessel moving roughly in the right direction. All being well, however, there were actually five positions from which the ship could be steered: bridge, two positions on the conning tower, and two on the signal tower.

Electrical systems

Dreadnought and its kin were huge physical entities, requiring prodigious amounts of electrical power to sustain their numerous functions. Principal electrical generation was provided by four Siemens dynamos, two of them driven by Brotherhood steam piston engines and two by Mirrlees diesel engines (although one of the diesel engines was replaced by a steam engine prior to commissioning, following reliability issues). These engines and dynamos could be run when

the ship was not under power, such as when in harbour, and then generated a total power output of 410kW, according to John Roberts's *The Battleship Dreadnought*, 'supplying current at 1000 amps and connected in parallel to a Cowan switchboard from which the 100-volt circuits were distributed on a branch system' (Roberts, p. 27). The dynamos were thunderous pieces of equipment, the steam-powered version weighing a total of 8.5 tons, while the larger diesel-powered unit weighed 17 tons. Both ran at 400rpm.

The dreadnoughts and super dreadnoughts became increasingly hungry in terms of electrical consumption, resulting in a steady

BELOW Engineers diligently tend the powerplant of HMS *Royal Oak*, with power supplied by 18 Babcock and Wilcox boilers generating 40,000shp.

increase in generating capacity. For example, while the *Dreadnought* had a total output of 400kW, the later *Queen Elizabeth* could produce 700kW, by virtue of two 200kW turbo-generators and two 150kW diesels at 220 volts DC. By the time we get to the *King George V* class of super dreadnought, we see each ship fitted with no fewer than eight 300kW generators (six turbo and two diesel), together delivering a total of 2,400kW of power. A key point to note in the development of dreadnought electrical power is that in 1905 the 200-volt ring main system was introduced into warship design. *Dreadnought* was intended as a beneficiary of this design, but as it happened the adoption did not take place until the *Bellerophon*-class vessels.

Dreadnought also had an extensive 15-volt DC low-power system fitted throughout the ship. John Roberts explains:

[this] consisted of a number of motor generators to supply 15-volt DC circuits via two switchboards – one in the main switchboard room and one in the 'X' turret working space. These supplied the fire control instruments, gun firing circuits and other communication devices. Later, a third lower-power switchboard was fitted in the 12-pdr working space on the lower deck, the gun circuits being separated from the cabin bell, revolution indicator and other minor circuits which were run entirely off the board in the main starboard room. In addition to these a separate motor generator was fitted for the telephone exchange, and motor alternators (DC–AC converters) were provided for the wireless transmitters and turret danger signals.

Roberts, *The Battleship Dreadnought*

Dreadnought's life, and indeed that of any battleship of this era, depended upon the delivery of electrical power, once hand power and steam-driven mechanical power began to recede into the past. Electrical power had to be applied to all manner of purposes – refrigeration, lighting, hoists lifting everything from shells to boats, the telephone communications, wireless transmissions, pumps and compressors, heating, powered workshop tools and much more. In fact, a large dreadnought-type vessel might have in the region of 400 electrical drive motors dotted around above and below decks.

Some elements of *Dreadnought*'s electrical systems were more important than others, such as navigational compasses. By December 1906, *Dreadnought* had been fitted with three compasses, located on the bridge, compass platform and the quarterdeck. Three types of

RIGHT The compass platform of HMS *Rodney*, a *Lord Nelson*-class battleship.

LEFT A perspective
of the tripod foremast
on HMS *Dreadnought*.
Funnel smoke ingress
into the foretop
was a problem for
Dreadnought and
some others of her
type.

compass were fitted: standard, liquid and a Siemens electrical, the first two being basic naval compasses but the latter being the only example of its type fitted to a Royal Navy warship. The electric compass was designed to provide better integration with the ship's fire-control systems, but in practice it did not perform well, so from 1911 it was replaced by a variety of gyro-compasses.

The other two compasses provided satisfactory service, although the Experimental Cruise threw up a few problems. With the standard compass, there was some deviation caused by the electromechanical interference of the ship's own magnetic character, but adjustments made at Trinidad appeared to solve the most serious of the worries. Regarding the Pattern 23 liquid compass, the main difficulties for this instrument came from the blast of gunfire, which shattered the plate glass on the binnacle helmet, and from the vibrations of the ship under way. The Experimental Cruise report noted:

It is suggested that the method of suspension is not strong enough to support a compass of such weight when subjected to excessive vibration, and that a more efficient one would be to support the outer gimbal ring by stout spiral springs, on the same principle as the Kelvin's pontoon compass.

R.C. Bacon, *Report on the Experimental Cruise*, 1907

For communications, *Dreadnought* had a variety of internal and inter-ship systems fitted during its lifetime. The critical engineering and operational spaces were linked by a central telephone exchange located on the lower deck, through which could flow a total of 46 connections and 3 extensions. There were also direct-connection navyphones

RIGHT On a British super dreadnought, wireless aerials run down from the tops to a fitting point behind the forward turrets.

making important individual auditory links between, for example, fire-control positions and between machinery compartments. John Roberts notes in *The Battleship Dreadnought*, that while in the *Dreadnought* 'exchange lamps and call bells were supplied with power from a motor-generator but the speaking circuits were powered by batteries'; in later dreadnoughts all parts of the system were generator-powered.

Looking to the battleship's wireless systems, its first fitment was the venerable Tune C Mk II set, which had an inter-ship transmission range of between 250 and 500 miles. An improved version (the Type 1) was introduced in 1911, plus a low-power, short-range Type 3 (also known as the Short Distance Set), which was intended as a replacement for flag signalling. In 1917, the wireless configuration was updated with the addition of the Type 16 auxiliary set and Type 13 after-action set, then the following year with the Type 31 fire-control set. Across the spectrum of such devices, *Dreadnought* and similar vessels had reasonable wireless communication across distances of a few hundred metres up to hundreds of miles, although visual means (flags, signal lamps, etc.) remained common at short ranges.

Ventilation and cooling

The topic of ventilation and cooling was a critical one in warship design during the first half of the 20th century. It could be one of those intensely practical aspects overlooked or under-appreciated at the initial design stages. For those who had to live with the reality of poorly ventilated spaces, however, the designer's lack of investment could result in truly dreadful living conditions. Following the Experimental Cruise, the following observations were made about the ship's ventilation issues:

1. *The following places are not ventilated, and require a supply of air:–*
    Lower conning tower.
    Lower signal tower.
    Lamp-room.
    Chief of staff's office.
    Electric store and acid room.
    W.R. officers' smoking-room.

LEFT An air intake cowl and weather flap, giving an air velocity in the shaft of 30ft/sec to the rooms below decks.

2. *The following spaces are inadequately ventilated:–*
    Mess decks.
    Electricians' and armourers' workshop.
    Engineers' store-room.
    Switchboard-room. (An improved trunk would rectify this.)
3. *To improve the ventilation of the main deck larger fans (say 20-in.) and larger trunks should be fitted, and if possible the trunks should be led with less bends, and the necessary bends made more gradual. Most of the air in the supply is wasted through the first few louvres and branches. These should be made smaller than the more remote ones.*
4. *The 12½-in. propeller fans used as exhaust fans for the seaman's head are not really necessary.*

R.C. Bacon, *Report on the Experimental Cruise*, 1907

Reading between the lines here, we can see how important ventilation was to maintaining the efficiency of the ship and the health of its personnel. In the list of affected spaces in points 1 and 2, we see several workshop and storage spaces that, with absent or poor ventilation, could become thick with toxic gases, or at least with overwhelming heat. Furthermore, a lack of ventilation was also a mechanical issue – an absence of moving fresh air would result in the build-up of corrosive condensation on sensitive electrical parts. Even more problematic could be the concern that excessive build-up of heat could result in machinery, such as generators and dynamos, overheating and breaking down.

These mechanical worries became even more profound when considering the sheer importance of keeping the boiler rooms fed with fresh air, both to improve the efficiency of the engines and keep the formidable heat of the spaces under control. Two editions and two reprints of the volume *The Air Supply to Boiler Rooms of Modern Ships of War* were published between 1916 and 1921, exploring in detail the physical challenges of delivering air to boilers. The author of the 1921 edition, Richard W. Allen, makes the point that boiler ventilation, particularly on oil-fired ships, was a fundamental consideration for ship performance:

It is a well-known fact that in burning oil fuel, higher air pressures are required than for coal, and consequently the power absorbed by the fans is considerable. Any improvement which can be effected by increasing the efficiency of the system, with a consequent saving in steam consumption, reduction in weight and space occupied,

will have some influence on the speed and economy of the ship.
Allen, *Air Supply to Boiler Rooms*

The author also notes in passing an academic factor that was a partial explanation of the problems reported on the capital ships:

When passing in review the difficulty of guiding the air into the entrances and through the downtakes, with the least possible resistance, as well as the question of the distribution of air in the stokeholds, one is forced to the conclusion that only the fringe of this important subject has been touched, especially having regard to the growth of the naval units during the last four years, and the great increase in the power of their propelling machinery, calling for much larger quantities of air to be delivered to the fans.
Allen, *Air Supply to Boiler Rooms*

Dreadnought's most visible ventilation ducts clung to the sides of the two funnels, each running down to a fan chamber supplying the boiler rooms. Below decks, the ship's ventilation was delivered through similar supply trunks fitted with electric fans, plus the usual variety of apertures that could be opened to allow the passage of fresh air. Regarding the trunks, the

RIGHT Here we see two fan blades used in battleship ventilation systems, giving a striking impression of their size.

desirable air speed flowing through was 20–25ft/ sec, although in some instances up to 48ft/sec might be preferable when heavier air flow was required. The key to effective trunking design was to provide an unimpeded air flow through the intake, then to channel that air flow through to the required space without slowing it down through too many sharp corners and obstructions.

Dreadnought's problem was partly a lack of adequate ventilation, but also somewhat due to the fact that hundreds of yards of steam pipes ran through the ship's spaces, acting like a vast central heating system even when it wasn't required. According to John Roberts's book *The Battleship Dreadnought*, a primary modification after the Experimental Cruise was the fitting of 'exhaust fans to the escape trunks of the dynamo rooms and the forward hydraulic engine rooms (the after hydraulic engine room was considered satisfactory). These alterations were carried out between August and November 1907, when a 25in electrically-driven exhaust fan was fitted on the main deck of each of the three escape trunks concerned.' (Roberts, p. 27).

Another problem that had to be addressed following the Experimental Cruise was the temperatures reached in the ship's cordite magazines. The report stated: 'The ventilation of the magazines is not good enough for a hot climate, and the temperature reached 100° Fahr., which is excessive, and detrimental to the cordite.' At high physical temperatures, the cordite could start to fragment chemically, resulting in less consistent burn qualities when fired. The powder could also become more unstable, raising the risk of accidental detonations. To resolve this issue, *Dreadnought*'s magazines each received a ventilation system through which cooled air was delivered from one of two steam-driven carbon dioxide cooler plants. These reduced the temperature of the magazine spaces to a more stable 80°F.

Dreadnought was a complicated entity, but overall it was essentially a reliable instrument of war, capable of sailing thousands of miles and fighting along the way. That all the other dreadnoughts and super dreadnoughts also 'carried the message' dependably across the world is a testimony to the shipbuilding capabilities of the British nation.

ABOVE AND LEFT
Two types of steam turbine-gear-driven warship fan, designed in 1918–19.

Chapter Five

The crew and their responsibilities

The dreadnoughts and super dreadnoughts were living communities. With complements exceeding the population of a small village, they required organisation and good working relations to ensure that they operated smoothly and coherently.

OPPOSITE *Dreadnought*'s wardroom, as seen in 1906, demonstrating the relative levels of luxury in which the officers could spend their downtime.

RIGHT A photograph
demonstrating that
everyone starts at the
bottom. Future Admiral
John Fisher, seen here
as an acting mate in
1860. (NMRN)

FAR RIGHT 'Scatters',
another of the
Dreadnought cats,
seen here with an
affectionate rating,
who is wearing
standard navy blues.

OPPOSITE A poster
illustrating the sheer
cost of a dreadnought
when compared
against other
military purchases.
The expense of
dreadnought
production raised
some concern among
other branches of the
armed services.

*When a number of people have to live and
work together, there must be rules and
discipline if they are to live comfortably and
to work properly. At school there is a time for
everything, and punctuality is a virtue which
is its own reward, though lack of it involves
penalties. This school is divided one way
for work, another for games, and another
for eating and sleeping. That is the school
routine, and routine is even more necessary
on board ship.*

The Wonder Book of the Navy

This quotation, although published in a
children's book in the 1920s, is a useful lead-in
to this chapter's theme. First, the fact that the
book was a children's volume did not separate
it too distinctly from the concern of many
serving sailors who were, after all, often in their
mid- to late teens. Second, the comparison to
a school is guiding. Schools, just like warships,
partly thrive on one particular quality – order –
often embodied in deeply engrained routines
and buttressed by an *esprit de corps*. On
a warship, order was transmitted through
a sharp understanding of each crewman's
responsibilities and duties, and how those
commitments connected with those of others.
Only once this order was in place, overseen
with trickle-down efficiency from the captain and
senior officers, could the vessel be expected to
function properly. Moreover, this was not just a
matter of pedantry – it was rather a matter of
life and death. The warship that had a strongly
embedded sense of practical integration was
likely to respond to the traumas of combat with
a more robust spirit, and the crew was less
likely to lose composure under fire.

In total, *Dreadnought* had a crew of about
770 men. By the end of the super dreadnought
age, the complement of Royal Navy battleships
would be more in the region of 1,100–1,200. Yet
regardless of the size of the complement, it was
imperative that the crew could perform the ship's
functions fluidly and quickly, practising in peace
what they might have to do for real in war.

On 31 March 1908, the Admiralty Intelligence
Department published its regular *Complements
of H.M. Ships* document. This document,
like all other similar publications, broke down
by role the complements assigned to each
major warship. As such, it forms a useful
document for understanding the functions and
composition of the crew aboard *Dreadnought*.
As in some previous chapters, the focus here
is squarely on HMS *Dreadnought*, yet the data
provided on other vessels, such as *Bellerophon*
and *St Vincent*, shows that the crew principles

and allocations applied to *Dreadnought* were common among many of the Navy's capital vessels. Usefully, the document also breaks down the crew into sub-grouped branches, and the analysis that follows conforms to this structure. Note that the total complement for the *Dreadnought* at this particular point in time was 724.

Military Branch

The first category in the *Complements of H.M. Ships* is the Military Branch (today this would be referred to as the Warfare Branch). As we shall see, this was a very broad category, running from the captain at the top down to the lowliest boy. Taken as a whole it was the largest of the branches, essentially responsible for the fundamental operational performance of the ship in both peace and war, and the delivery of all its essential functions.

The summit of the Military Branch on

Dreadnought was naturally occupied by its senior command roles, with the captain and commander supported by the listed officers:

Lieutenant, R.N.	6
for Gunnery duties	1
for Torpedo duties	1
Commander N., or Lieutenant N.	1
Sub-Lieutenant, R.N.	3

Together this body of men would essentially form the command 'brain' of the warship, the officers beneath the captain responsible for filtering down the captain's major decisions through the decks and structures below. The rest of the Military Branch crewmen were a mix of distinct technical specialisms and general seamen. Regarding the former, the specialisms were chiefly focused on gunnery and communications. In addition to two chief gunners and one chief gunner for torpedo duties, the *Complements* document lists positions of gunner's mate, gunlayer (1st, 2nd and 3rd class), torpedo gunner's mate, leading torpedo man plus 122 other personnel devoted to manning and maintaining the ship's armament. Communications specialists included two telegraphists plus the following personnel listed for 'Signals':

Chief Signal Boatswain	1
Yeoman	4
2nd Yeoman, O.S./Leading Signalman	7
Signalman	6
Ordinary Signalman, or Signal Boy	8

One other specialist who deserves mention for being listed is that of sailmaker, one of which was listed in *Dreadnought*'s complement. Although the days of sail had long since disappeared, even the modern battleship had substantial volumes of canvas and other sheet materials around the ship, all of which needed maintenance and repair. Even into the Second World War we find the role of sailmaker appearing in some ship's complement lists.

Specialist gunners and communications personnel would often have had a very intimate connection to the decision-making processes of the ship. Many of the more senior specialists would work side by side with the captain in the

bridge, helping to ensure that commands were supported by technical knowledge, and that messages were effectively flowed throughout the ship and indeed across to other ships. Others, however – here the torpedo men spring to mind – would rarely see the light of day, labouring away well below the main deck.

The bulk of the Military Branch, however, was made up of the far more numerous groups of men who performed myriad general duties. Of the more senior – the equivalent of NCOs – were 18 midshipmen officer cadets, 22 petty officers, 13 2nd class petty officers and 13 leading seamen. They would have had face-

ABOVE A battleship crew collect around the forward armament for a ceremonial photograph. Dreadnought and super dreadnought complements ranged from about 750 to nearly 1,200 men.

NAVAL INSTRUCTIONS

Journal and Note Book for the Use of Junior Officers:

1 The Journal is to be kept during the whole of the Midshipman's sea-time. A second journal may be issued if required.

2 The Lieutenant detailed to supervise the Midshipmen's instruction is to be responsible that the Journal is properly kept. It is to be sent to the Captain once a month and initialled by him.

3 The Journal is intended to be neither a copy of the Ship's Log nor a personal

diary. It is intended rather to contain notes on points of special interest connected with a Naval Officer's professional duties, so that when completed it may form a useful book of reference. Midshipmen should be encouraged to cultivate their own powers of observation; for this reason the Journal should not as a rule be used for dictated or copied notes.

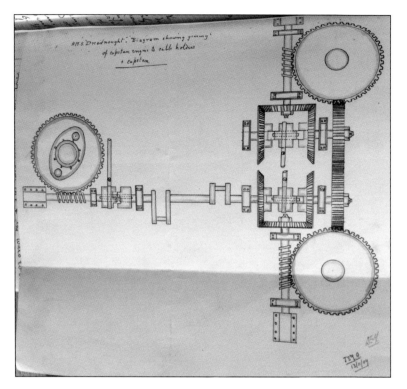

ABOVE Signalmen sort out the compartments of signal flags. Signalmen were often known as 'bunting tossers' by the rest of the crew.

ABOVE AND BELOW The midshipman's log was an important record of the officer cadet's comprehension of shipboard life. Here we see two beautiful technical illustrations in the log of Midshipman John St Erme Cardew.

to-face contact with the most sizeable bodies of sailors aboard *Dreadnought*, the 220 able/ordinary seamen and 32 boys, 1st class. The latter had entered naval service around the age of 15½, serving for up to 18 months as a 'boy, 2nd class' before being promoted to 1st class status between the ages of 16 and 18. Once he hit the age of 18, he would be classified as an ordinary seaman.

Before moving on to look at the Engineering Branch, it is worth exploring one of these positions in more detail, if only for the unique

records that these personnel kept. Midshipmen were essentially officers in training. Although destined for the higher ranks, their journey up to that position actually meant starting pretty much at the bottom. Messing conditions could be haphazard and rudimentary, and they would also become familiar with the humble seamen's outlook, humour and priorities. Such is what made the midshipman position a good apprenticeship for future service. What is particularly useful for historians is the journal that such men were obliged to keep, the purpose and criteria of which is explained in the feature box on the previous page. For *Dreadnought* we have a particularly useful resource in the journal kept by John St Erme Cardew, Midshipman Royal Navy, while serving on board *Dreadnought*, *Defence* and *Beagle*. The following extract from this journal, written in the autumn of 1909, is not only useful for seeing *Dreadnought* through the eyes of one particular midshipman, it is also insightful for getting a sense of the general life cycle of the ship:

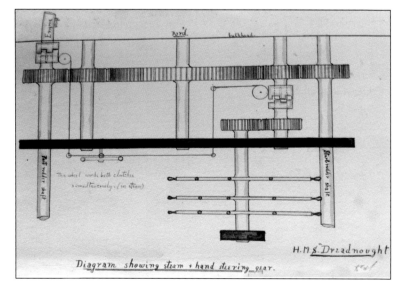

Thurs. Sept. 16th
6.30am
Joined HMS Dreadnought. Shown around the ship. Went outside during the forenoon practising for night defence. Anchored at noon. Weighed anchor 8 p.m. and proceeded to practise for night defence. The principles of night defence are to test the ability of a ship to hit another ship under the following conditions,

1) Ability to hit a single boat as soon as possible after the searchlights have been switched on. 2nd [sic] The ability to discover another ship and engage with her <u>without</u> searchlights. 3rd. The ability to discover and engage with ships <u>with</u> searchlights. The tests were carried [out] in four ways. 1) Firing at torpedo boat target towed by another ship. 2) This is the same as (1) only other guns are brought to bear on the target. 3) Discovering and engaging with targets moored at sea without the use of searchlights. 4) This is the same as (3) only searchlights are used. In tests 1 + 2 the range can be anything between 800 [and] 12,000 yards; Tests 3 + 4 must not be less than 2,000 yards. In many cases the time limit is 2 minutes after the target has first been seen.

Frid. 17th
Proceeded to Galspia(?) bay and anchored there during the forenoon. Having taken aboard umpires for night defence competition, at 8 p.m. weighed anchor and proceeded to carry out the test already stated above. Anchored at 12.30 p.m. in Dornoch(?) bay.

Sat. 18th
At 5 a.m. the next morning we weighed anchor and proceeded to Cromarty Firth. There was a low lying mist all around but it did not hinder the navigation of the ship. We moored in our usual billet.

Sunday 19th
In the afternoon a footer match was arranged between ourselves and the Bellerophon and resulted in a victory for us after a hard-fought

game. Sunday being wet divisions and church were held on the main deck.

Monday 20th
Several officers from the ship attended court martial held on board the Irresistible to try a chief petty of this ship for stealing. The case was not however proved and the prisoner was acquitted. During the afternoon watch, it was discovered, just in time, that the beef contractor had endeavoured to deposit some bags of potatoes and vegetables on the port after ladder. Fortunately a couple of hands were quick taking the goods back in the boat again just as it was shoving off. The skipper was furious, but he did not know the flag commander was on top just waiting for a boat to come alongside. The admiral gave a dance on the quarter deck which, from all accounts, was a great success. In the afternoon a serious accident occurred to one of the midshipmen of the King Edward VII. He fell off the cliffs at Nigg(?) and although at present he remains alive, he has fractured his skull badly.

In the space of just four days, we see the broad spectrum of life on board *Dreadnought*, from training in gunnery practice to dealing with disciplinary issues. Such accounts are useful for reminding us that the crews of the great dreadnoughts and super dreadnoughts spent the vast majority of their service life not in combat, but rather in the experience of running of a great ship, an end that was worthy in itself.

Engineer Branch

The roles and responsibilities of the Engineer Branch would appear to speak for themselves. The personnel of this branch were tasked with keeping the ship mechanically functional, particularly in relation to the powerplant, auxiliary machinery and electrical systems.

The 1908 *Complement* lists *Dreadnought*'s engineering personnel as follows:

Engineer Commander or Engineer Lieutenant of over 8 years' seniority	1
Engineer Lieutenant of less than 8 years' seniority, or Engineer Sub-Lieutenant	3
Chief Artificer Engineer or Artificer Engineer	2
Chief Engine Room Artificer	4
Engine Room Artificer	16
Chief Stoker	9
Mechanician	Up to 6
Stoker Petty Officer	14
Leading Stoker	14
Stoker	58

The technical skill and practical knowledge embodied in these personnel was truly extensive. Naturally officers and artificers connected to the engine room were experts in all matters relating to *Dreadnought*'s powerplant and to naval propulsion, but even those lower down the rankings had to wield considerable know-how. For example, and looking outside the Royal Navy documentation momentarily, the US Navy's *Naval Artificer's Manual* of 1914 indirectly explains the scope of the engineer's role aboard a warship by describing the content of the manual:

> *Appertaining to the care and preservation of the hull and fittings, and the operation of auxiliary machinery on ships of the Navy. Containing elementary arithmetic, rules and tables of weights, measures, etc., weights and strengths of materials, rules for inspection of and descriptions of all kinds of lumber used in the Navy; descriptions of drainage, sanitary and ventilation systems, steering appliances including telemotors, oxy-acetylene welding etc.; standard formulae for mixing all kinds of paints used on iron and steel vessels. Examination questions pertaining to the different trades of Deck Artificers, glossary of technical and nautical definitions, etc.*

It is difficult to think of any equivalent civilian professions in which the engineer would have to range across such a spectrum of technical knowledge. The US manual itself stretches to 824 pages of close information, and the

artificers of all other world navies would have also had to display similar broad and specific awareness. Given the physical complexity of a dreadnought, engineering personnel were in constant demand, even when the ship was essentially running without major problems. A taste of the engineer's life can be taken from a 1907 diary of the Experimental Cruise. Here the engineering challenges of just a few days are selected:

4th January
New armature fitted port engine, ran in presence of officers, satisfactory, fly wheel true, bearing cool. Ran from 8.30 p.m. until 2 p.m. on 6th January (41½ hours).

6th January
Port engine started at 10.30 p.m. Starboard engine range for 5 hours.

7th January
10 p.m., after running for 21½ hours, armature spider fractured, and boltheads sheared, flywheel partly off its spigot.

10th January
Starboard engine stopped at 10 a.m. of its own accord. Found spindle of rotary oil fuel pump fractured. Fitted space spindle and restarted. Stopped at 10.30 p.m. Note. – Proposed to make new rotary pump spindle of steel. Proposed to make oil overflow level lower in cam-shaft channel to diminish oil splashing.

14th January
Starboard engine running 15½ hours. Engine brought up. Found spindle of rotary oil fuel pump fractured. Fitted spare and restarted.

17th–18th January
Overhauling generally. Cleaned valve gear, took adjustments, repacked glands of oil fuel pump. Examined H.P. suction valves of air compressor.
R.C. Bacon, *Report on the Experimental Cruise*, 1907

As these entries suggest, engineers worked long hours, and had to turn their minds to some

ABOVE This impression of the stoker's life manages to be both idealised and grimy. Heavy ventilation to the boiler rooms was required both for mechanical efficiency and for the crew's health.

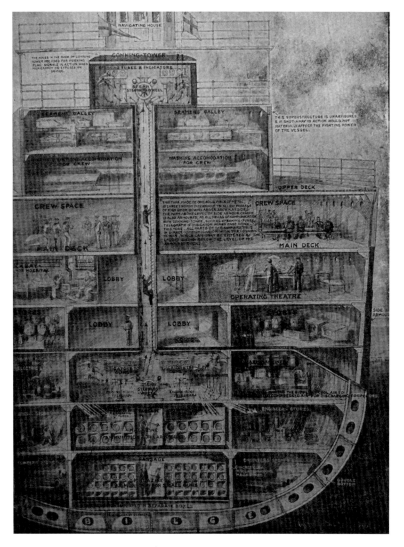

LEFT This illustration displays how the super dreadnought's conning tower section is laid out. Although not totally accurate, it gives a useful impression of crew spaces and movement.

heavy-duty mechanical work at unpredictable times of the day.

Even the humble stokers, the most numerous of the personnel in the Engineering Branch, were a long way from being simple manual labourers. Their work was certainly unglamorous, labouring endlessly down in a filthy room, half choked on coal dust and fumes, shovelling hundreds of pounds of coal from coal rooms to furnaces. Yet the 1912 manual that accompanied their trade was itself a substantial volume, with complex information about the operation and science behind boilers and their relation to engine function. Even the simple matter of making a boiler fire and raising steam was not straightforward:

> *Raising Steam. – Lay and wood fires and light fires up when ordered. See that the dampers are open, the draught plates shut and furnace doors open.*
>
> *See nothing inflammable is on top or at the sides of the boiler.*
>
> *In cylindrical boilers where the furnaces are not on the same level, light the lower furnaces first so as to gradually heat the boiler.*
>
> *Steam should always be raised slowly in cylindrical boilers and also in water-tube boilers where the brickwork is new or recently repaired, if the service allows, but at other times, when urgently required, steam may be raised in water-tube boilers more rapidly.*
>
> *Time should always be allowed, however, to properly warm the engines.*
>
> *When the front of the fire is thoroughly burnt through push it back with the rake over the unlighted part of the coal, and lightly*

LEFT At visual ranges semaphore signalling was still used into the Second World War era, although after Jutland the improvement of short-range wireless communications was recommended.

*sprinkle coal over the furnace. Shut the
furnace door and open the draught plates.*

*The fire should be kept as thin as possible
and without holes while raising steam and
until the engines are under way; this will
guard against blowing off and will also
prevent the fire-bars from becoming warped
and bent.*

The Stoker's Manual

Artisan Branch

The Artisan Branch was another specialist
technical section of the Royal Navy ships,
with responsibilities that didn't quite stretch up
to the major mechanical components of the
vessel, but which nevertheless were still critical
to the ship's function. In essence they were the
manual tradesmen of the ship, and their titles
from the *Dreadnought* complement are fairly
self-explanatory:

Chief Carpenter or Carpenter	1
Carpenter's Mate	2
Leading Shipwright	3
Shipwright	2
Leading Carpenter's Crew	2
Carpenter's Crew	4
Blacksmith	1
Blacksmith's Mate	2
Plumber	1
Plumber's Mate	1
Painter, 1st Class	1
Painter, 2nd Class	1
Cooper or 2nd Cooper	1
Cooper's Crew	1
Chief Armourer	1
Armourer's Mate	1
Armourer's Crew	2
Electrician	6

What is most striking about this list
is its comprehensive reach. It is evident
from the range of skills offered here that
dreadnoughts truly were self-contained
communities of endeavour, with all
the familiar civilian trades applied to a
naval context. Thus the ship includes
blacksmiths, coopers, painters, electricians
and plumbers, as well as more traditional

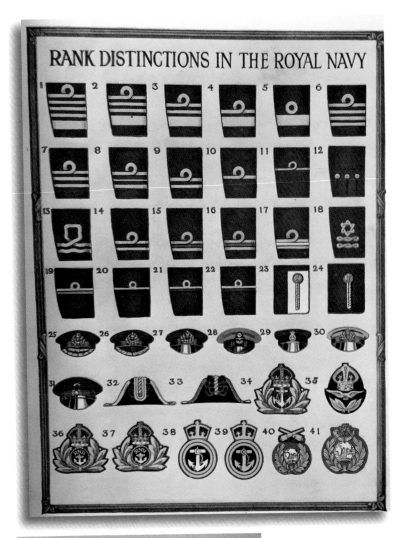

RANK DISTINCTIONS IN THE ROYAL NAVY

**DISTINCTIONS OF RANK IN THE
ROYAL NAVY**

Key to Coloured Plates.

SLEEVES

1. Admiral of the Fleet.
2. Admiral.
3. Vice-Admiral.
4. Rear-Admiral and Commodore, 1st Class.
5. Commodore, 2nd Class.
6. Captain.
7. Commander.
8. Lieutenant-Commander.
9. Lieutenant.
10. Sub-Lieutenant, Mate, and Commissioned Warrant Officer.
11. Warrant Officers (non-military Warrant Officers wear in addition a strip of distinction cloth as Nos. 19 to 22).
12. Midshipman (mess jacket).
13. Lieutenant, Royal Naval Volunteer Reserve.
14. Engineer Lieutenant. All Engineer Officers wear a stripe or stripes of *purple* cloth between the gold bands of their rank.
15. Surgeon Lieutenant. Medical Officers wear *red* stripes between the gold bands.
16. Instructor Lieutenant. Instruction Officers wear *light blue* stripes.
17. Paymaster Lieutenant. Paymasters wear *white* stripes.
18. Lieutenant, Royal Naval Reserve.
19. Shipwright (silver grey strip).
20. Wardmaster (maroon strip).
21. Electrician (dark green strip).
22. Armourer or Ordnance (dark blue strip).
23. Midshipman's "patch," R.N.
24. Naval cadet's "patch," R.N.

CAPS

25. Flag Officers.
26. Captains and Commanders.
27. All other Officers.
28. Captain, Royal Air Force.
29. Chief Petty Officer.
30. Lieutenant, Royal Naval Division.
31. Royal Marine Artillery.
32. Flag Officer's Cocked Hat (full dress).
33. Lieutenant's Cocked Hat (full dress).

CAP BADGES.

34. All Executive Officers.
35. Royal Air Force.
36. Royal Naval Reserve.
37. Royal Naval Volunteer Reserve.
38. Petty Officer, Executive Branch.
39. Petty Officer, Civil Branch.
40. Royal Marine Artillery.
41. Royal Marine Infantry.

ABOVE AND LEFT
**A presentation of
'Distinctions of Rank
in the Royal Navy', and
its corresponding key.**

ABOVE A battleship has its hull paintwork refreshed.

RIGHT In poor weather, sailors launch one of the battleship's small boats, a potentially dangerous duty with many opportunities for crushed limbs or falls overboard.

maritime professions such as shipwrights and military technicians like the armourers.

Medical Branch

The Medical Branch of a warship was responsible for the health, hygiene and medical treatment of the crew. They were invariably kept active. Even in peacetime, there would have been an endless litany of accidents and illnesses to contend with, the inevitable consequence of close life aboard a ship replete with dangerous equipment, slippery ladders and munitions. *Dreadnought*'s medical facilities would have permitted the medical team to perform all manner of surgery and disease treatment, although for very serious issues the preference was naturally for transfer to a land-based hospital as soon as possible.

The medical team would also be the centre of information about general health practices. A huge problem in the Navy at this time, as evidenced by contemporary naval medical reports, was venereal disease contracted during shore leave. More than 50% of medical issues could be related to afflictions like gonorrhoea and syphilis. Other common illness such as tuberculosis, plus tropical ailments like malaria, meant the ship's medical quarters remained busy.

The Medical Branch personnel listed for *Dreadnought* in 1908 were:

Fleet of Staff Surgeon or Surgeon	1
Surgeon	2
Chief S.B. Steward	1
Second S.B. Steward	1
S.B. Attendant	1

Other branches

An often overlooked but critical component of the ship's crew was the Accountant Branch, headed by the paymaster and assisted by a small team of assistants, clerks and writers. This team would oversee the financial arrangements of the ship, from the crew's pay through to the purchase of food and other supplies when in port. Notably, many of the ship's cooking personnel are listed under the Accountant Branch, doubtless because their efforts depended upon sound management of the food budget and their effective use of the stores. The cookery personnel listed for *Dreadnought* are:

Chief Ship's Cook	2
Ship's Cook	1
Leading Cook's Mate	3
Cook's Mate or 2nd Cook's Mate	4

There was also a separate branch listed as 'Officers' Stewards and Cooks'. Within this category, 1st, 2nd and 3rd class stewards/cooks were assigned to the commanding officer, ward room, gun room and warrant officers, ensuring that the upper hierarchy of the ship was well served and entertained.

Battleships of the dreadnought era would also usually have a complement of Royal Marines on board, separated into artillery and infantry. The purpose of the Royal Marines was to provide

RIGHT A ship's cook prepares his produce. On a ship such as a super dreadnought, overall food consumption could be 7–10 tons per day.

on-shore combat duty and also ship-boarding capabilities when required. A small wheeled artillery piece would usually be held within the ship for use by the Marine artillery trooper.

BELOW A team on HMS *Revenge* man the High-Angle Control System (HACS), which was used to calculate deflection for anti-aircraft shooting. HACS was fitted to *Revenge* in the 1930s.

In 1908, *Dreadnought*'s Marines were led by one major or captain plus a lieutenant. The rest of the troops broke down as follows:

Artillery	
Sergeant	1
Corporal, or Bombardier	3
Bugler	1
Gunner	26
Infantry	
Sergeant	1
Corporal	2
Bugler	1
Private	26

The buglers listed here were not the only musical element of the ship's company. There would also be a ship's band, which for *Dreadnought* in 1908 consisted of:

Bandmaster, 1st Class	1
Band Corporal	1
Musician	13

The band would have both ceremonial and entertainment duties, and the individual members were of necessity versatile musicians. On one occasion they might be playing a stately waltz for visiting dignitaries and their wives, while on others they might be whipping up lively popular tunes for the men.

Some of the final, and interesting, members of the ship's complement worth mentioning include 'Private as Butcher', 'Private as Lamp Trimmer', 'Diver' and 'Tailor'.

As this journey through *Dreadnought*'s company shows, every warship in the Royal Navy, and those of other navies, contained a wealth of talent, experience, intelligence and technical skill. Although the steel and wood of the ship provided the fabric for power projection, it was only the abilities of such men that brought that tool to life.

Chapter Six

Dreadnoughts in war and peace

The dreadnoughts and super dreadnoughts without doubt dominated the global arms race of the 1910s and 1920s. Yet despite such powerful ships, and for such enormous financial investment, their historical influence would be all too brief.

OPPOSITE *Dreadnought* presents a fine view of the starboard quarter in harbour. Coaling derricks are extended either side of the mainmast. *(NMRN)*

ABOVE The *Queen Elizabeth*-class super dreadnought HMS *Barham* ploughs through the waves in the company of its sister ship *Malaya* and the aircraft carrier *Argus*.

On 25 November 1941, the *Queen Elizabeth*-class super dreadnought HMS *Barham* was steaming in the Mediterranean north of Sidi Barrani, Egypt, accompanied by *Queen Elizabeth* herself and another battleship of the class, *Valiant*. Together these three mighty ships plus eight destroyers constituted 'Force K', hunting Axis supply convoys attempting to make runs between Italy and North Africa. It must have projected a sense of impregnability, a vision of iron muscle on the Mediterranean waters, but that confidence was about to be torn apart.

At 4.25pm, and at just 750yd distance from *Barham*, Oberleutnant zur See Hans-Diedrich von Tiesenhausen, the commander of U-boat *U-331*, ordered a spread of torpedoes to be fired at the hulking targets in front of him. Three of them slammed into *Barham*, impacting close together and rending open the hull. As tens of thousands of gallons of seawater rushed into the now-stricken vessel, *Barham* began capsizing to port, dozens of men sliding down or clinging on to the hull. This horrifying development was filmed by Pathé cameraman John Turner, aboard HMS *Valiant*, who also caught what happened next. Just as the foremast settled into the water, *Barham* was virtually obliterated in a thunderous magazine explosion, splitting the ship in two and sending it quickly to the bottom. Within minutes, the only evidence of her existence was a dire pall of smoke hanging over the surface of the waters.

The fate of HMS *Barham*, sunk by a vessel a fraction of its size and cost, was emblematic of just how much naval warfare had changed in such a short space of time. Back in 1906, when *Dreadnought* was emerging on to the world scene, battleships were the true kings of the waves – the most Herculean warships yet conceived. Over the course of three decades, however, it became apparent that first submarines and then naval aircraft were the new hunters on the oceans, and battleships were almost unmissably big targets. During the Second World War, that lesson was learned to such an extent that post-war battleships almost entirely disappeared from fleet compositions.

RIGHT The catastrophic magazine explosion of HMS *Barham* on 25 November 1941, as witnessed by a Pathé film crew.

RIGHT HMS *Royal Oak*'s sinking by a U-boat at Scapa Flow in 1939 shocked the naval establishment. In this photograph, note the prominent rangefinder behind 'B' turret.

The cruel experience of HMS *Barham*, which resulted in the deaths of 841 out of a crew of 1,184 men, was far from the first indication of this shift. On 14 October 1939, the *Revenge*-class battleship *Royal Oak* had been sunk by U-boat attack while supposedly safe at anchor in Scapa Flow, hit by a single torpedo fired by *U-47* and captained by the future U-boat ace Kapitänleutnant Günther Prien. Some 833 men died. It was an early and shocking wartime loss to the Royal Navy, and a sombre wake-up call to the vulnerability of these mighty warships.

PARTIAL TRANSCRIPT OF THE BOARD OF INQUIRY PROCEEDINGS INTO THE SINKING OF HMS *ROYAL OAK*

At 0116 the Captain was still near the C.O.2 room with several Officers. In his own words 'I had no thought other than that a local explosion had taken place in the Inflammable Store. This was backed up by the report I received that the C.O.2 room was intact. I had not even thought of the ship being torpedoed. I felt no uneasiness about the safety of the ship.' Suddenly there was another 'shattering' explosion, followed at very short intervals by a third and fourth. These explosions occurred on the starboard side of the ship approximately between 'A' and 'X' turrets, and had an immediate and catastrophic effect. The ship at once started to heel to starboard and, with only a slight 'hang' for perhaps three or four minutes, heeled over with increasing velocity until she capsized at 0129.

From the moment the second explosion occurred it was practically impossible to do anything effective to save the ship, nor was it possible to broadcast the order to 'Abandon Ship' as the lights went out and power failed. Officers in various parts of the ship told the men near them to save themselves. The Captain was still in the cable locker flat. He told Officers and men to clear out of the flat and walked aft to the Messdeck which was in darkness. He sent the men up to the forecastle and followed them up. On the forecastle he realised that the ship was going over as she was heeling so quickly and felt sure that the only thing left to do was to throw over the side the Carley floats etc. and as much wood as possible. The Captain and Commander got to work on this assisted by a few men, but, the ship turned over so rapidly that little could be done. In a few minutes they found the deck becoming impossible to stand on so climbed over the port guard rails and up the port side until they slipped or were flung into the sea.

The ship capsized and finally sank at 0129, twenty five minutes after the first explosion and thirteen minutes after the second explosion. An Officer who had climbed up the port side, over the bilge keel and onto the bottom checked the time at 0133 before taking to the water.

ADM 199/158, the record of the subsequent Board of Inquiry

H.M.S. DREADNOUGHT.

Under way

For now, we return to more confident times. Here it would be impossible to look at the operational life of each dreadnought and super dreadnought in detail. Instead, we will explore the life of *Dreadnought* herself in the pre-war period, then expand this analysis to examine the general service careers of all the great British dreadnoughts and super dreadnoughts during the world wars era.

Dreadnought was commissioned to full complement in December 1906. With the dawn of a new year, the first major voyage of her career was the aforementioned Experimental Cruise. This began on 5 January 1907 at Portsmouth and ended on 23 March in the same location, the great ship having journeyed to Spain, Gibraltar, Sardinia, Gibraltar again then across the Atlantic to Trinidad.

Prior to her heading out on this first voyage, it is worth noting that there was some Admiralty concern that the world's docks were not suited to handling such a sizeable vessel. On 9 October 1906, an official request went out to the Royal Navy Hydrographer, stating: 'The First Sea Lord would be glad if you would kindly let him have, as soon as possible, a list of the Docks, British and Foreign, that at present exist, capable of taking vessels of the "Dreadnought" size.' The reply came back:

Germany has one dock at Bremerhaven, one at Wilhelmshaven and 2 completing at the latter place that should be capable of taking a 'Dreadnought'.

France As far as our information goes there are no docks for 'Dreadnought' type. Toulon may have one but we have not sufficient complete dimensions to say positively; there is one building at Brest.

Italy Naples has a dock building that may possibly take a 'Dreadnought'.

Japan has one at Nagasaki.

America has one at San Francisco, and 3 building (Norfolk, Philadelphia, Brooklyn).

England One at Hebburn on Tyne. One at Southampton. One at Birkenhead (2 building). Possibly one at Liverpool and at Glasgow. One building at Belfast.

From this list it is understandable that *Dreadnought* was creating a new world of logistical issues, but those do not seem to have given much cause for concern during her Experimental Cruise.

A week's taste of the daily report on the Experimental Cruise provides not just a sense of

ABOVE The launch ceremony for HMS *Dreadnought* on 10 February 1906, appropriately performed by King Edward VII. *(NMRN)*

BELOW An interesting comparative newspaper feature from 1906, comparing *Dreadnought* with the USS *Connecticut*, suggests the impact of *Dreadnought* on naval thinking.

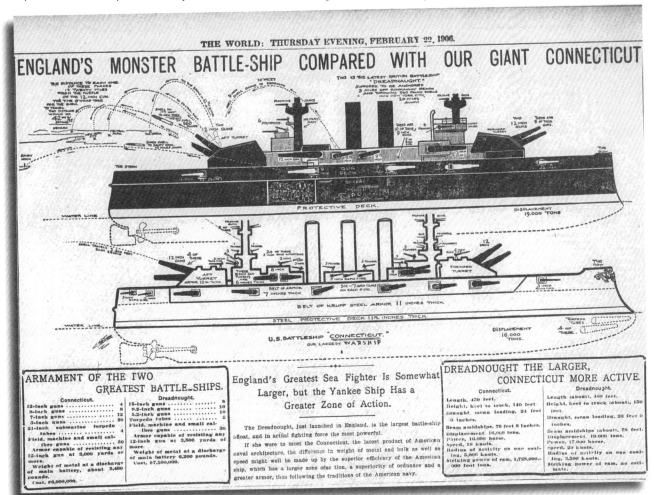

ABOVE One hundred
years of history
separate HMS
Victory, on the left in
Portsmouth harbour,
and *Dreadnought* as
she steams toward the
sea.

the ship finding its feet, but also of the general experience of daily life aboard a peacetime dreadnought during this era (table below).

The Experimental Cruise, and various other manoeuvres and trials in her first year of service, proved *Dreadnought* as a seaworthy vessel of good handling. A document entitled 'Secret, H.M.S. "Dreadnought" (Notes for use of the Parliamentary Secretary in Debate)' from this time gives several reassuring defences of the warship against her potential detractors:

The official turning trials showed that the 'Dreadnought' is, for a ship of her length, remarkable handy. Comparing her performances on trial and those of recently designed battleships, it is found that where the speeds are equal (12 knots) she turns on approximately the same circle as ships of the 'King Edward VII' class and on a smaller circle than earlier battleships of the 'Duncan,' 'Formidable,' and 'Canopus' classes,

Date	Drills, &c, carried out
Saturday, 5th January 1907. Spithead and at sea.	Sailed from Portsmouth, 8 a.m.
Monday, 7th January 1907. At sea and Arosa Bay.	3.40 p.m. – Arrived and anchored in Arosa Bay. Lieutenant Dreyer joined ship from 'Exmouth.'
Tuesday, 8th January 1907. Arosa Bay and at sea.	A.m. Exercised 'out port T.O. net defence' (1st time). Prepared ship for sea. P.m., 3.45 – Weighed and proceeded for Gibraltar.
Wednesday, 9th January 1907.	Hands employed in mustering bags. Preparing 12-pr. loader and deflection teachers. Clearing up magazines and shell rooms, &c.
Thursday, 10th January 1907. Gibraltar.	6.5 [*sic*] – Carried out turning trials. 9.0 a.m. – secured to Nos. 9 and 10 buoys, Gibraltar. Prepared ship for coaling. P.m. – Coal lighters came alongside.
Friday, 11th January 1907.	Coaled ship, 1,780 tons.
Saturday, 12th January 1907. Gibraltar.	Cleaned ship throughout after coaling. Took in oil from S.S. 'Petroleum.'
Monday, 14th January 1907. Gibraltar and at sea.	Prepared ship for sea. 11.10 – Slipped and proceeded for Aranci Bay. Y turret's crew and seven 12-prs. crews under instruction. Night – All searchlights, crew, and control parties exercised, burning searchlights.

although the latter are from 90 to 100 feet shorter than the 'Dreadnought.'

At a speed of 19 knots the 'Dreadnought's' tactical diameter is only 25 yards in excess of that of the 'King Edward VII' at 16 knots, and is smaller than that of the 'Duncan,' 'Formidable,' and 'Canopus' classes at speeds of from 15½ to 16½ knots.

But her handiness in open water, due to the smaller tactical diameter at all speeds, is not the only point in her favour. She showed none of that tendency to yaw and to be wild on her helm which is to be noticed not only in battleships but in the longer armoured cruisers; when swinging under helm, she was easily steadied by righting the helm when ¾ of a point off the course and meeting her with a few degrees of the opposite helm; it is the custom of all large ships to ease the helm from 1¼ to 1½ points off the course, and it is often necessary to employ as much as 15' of opposite helm to stop the swing and steady the ship.

When turning from rest under the screws she was also very handy and readily turned either up to or off the wind and sea, which is by no means a characteristic of the battleships and large cruisers built since 1890 and which have inward turning screws.

The report paints a favourable picture of the vessel's performance, although given the purpose of the document the reviewer is obviously loading his observation towards the lighter side. As we have seen at several points already in this book, the Experimental Cruise also highlighted a long list of issues that needed to be remedied.

From 1908 until 1914, Dreadnought passed her time in the same fashion as most other capital ships of this era. The naval year was usually spent conducting trials, manoeuvres and gunnery training; participating in reviews and strategic exercises with the wider fleet; and spending time in dock for repairs and refits. In terms of the ship's foreign adventures, in 1908 and 1909 she conducted strategic exercises and manoeuvres in the Atlantic with elements of the Home and Atlantic Fleets, and similar exercises with the Home, Atlantic and Mediterranean Fleets off the north-west coast of Spain in early 1911 and 1912. (Another landmark of 1912 was serving as a target tug in Bantry Bay for HMS Thunderer and Orion; Thunderer was in the process of testing out a new director system.) On 22 September 1913, Dreadnought sailed for the Mediterranean, where she remained for the rest of the year, conducting exercises with the 1st and 4th Battle

ABOVE *Dreadnought* **leads the Home Fleet to anchor at Spithead, honouring a pre-war visit by the King of Sweden.** *(NMRN)*

Squadrons and the 3rd Cruiser Squadron, among other events, before heading back to Britain in April 1914. Just three months later, *Dreadnought* and the rest of the Royal Navy's fleets would be at war.

Dreadnoughts at war: 1914–18

If we maintain a strict focus on dreadnoughts and super dreadnoughts, the ship-vs-ship combat experience gained by these vessels from the outset of the war until the Battle of Jutland in late May 1916 was fairly minimal. This is not to say that life was free from drama and incident. One heavy and early slap in the face for the British fleet was the loss of the *King George V*-class super dreadnought *Audacious*, on 27 October 1914. While conducting gunnery trials as part of the 2nd Battle Squadron near Tory Island off the coast of Donegal, the warship hit a single mine and began to take on water. The severity of the situation progressively became clear, and eight hours later the ship sank, thankfully with no loss of life. The fact that nothing more than a drifting mine had destroyed one of the Royal Navy's most potent battleships, however, can't have been lost on the Admiralty hierarchy.

ABOVE HMS *Audacious*, a *King George V*-class super dreadnought, showing a director control position on the foretop. *Audacious* was lost to a mine strike in 1914. *(LOC)*

There were also some early incidents with enemy submarines. On 8 August 1914, the *Orion*-class super dreadnought HMS *Monarch* dodged torpedoes fired at it from *U-15* near Fair Isle, the first such attack on a British battleship in the war. *Dreadnought* came even closer to a German U-boat on 18 March 1915. On that day *Dreadnought* was sailing home with the 4th Battle Squadron following exercises off Pentland Firth, when suddenly *U-29*, captained by Kapitänleutnant Otto Weddigen, broke surface ahead. The submarine had actually just fired a torpedo at HMS *Neptune* (the torpedo missed) and now found itself in the path of *Dreadnought*, which had set course to ram. The battleship squarely connected with the diminutive submarine, cutting *U-29* in half and sinking it with the loss of all hands. Apart from this action, however, *Dreadnought* was not really involved in the shooting war, and was undergoing a refit at the time of the Battle of Jutland.

German battleships also performed in a similar manner, the capital ships of the two fleets often keeping a wary distance. There were some significant clashes before Jutland. At the Battle of Dogger Bank on 24 January 1915, for example, the German battlecruisers *Seydlitz*, *Moltke*, *Derfflinger* and *Blücher* came to blows with Admiral David Beatty's Battlecruiser Force, consisting of *Lion*, *Tiger*, *Princess Royal*, *New Zealand* and *Indomitable*. (The order of battle also included a heavy cruiser presence on both sides, plus 18 torpedo boats on the German side, with the British being overall numerically superior.) The exchanges of fire began at 20,000yd – illustrating that the justifications for the big gun were definitely warranted. Both sides took some serious hits, but the German force came off the worse for the encounter, with *Blücher*

BELOW The German submarine *U-29*, captained by Otto Weddigen, leaves harbour in March 1915 on her last cruise – she was destroyed on 18 March after being rammed and sunk by *Dreadnought*.

ABOVE **The German battleship** *Moltke* **visits New York in 1912.** *Moltke* **was armed with 10 × 11in guns and was fast – the ship's designed speed was 25.5 knots.** *(LOC)*

sunk, although there were recriminations that Beatty's force had let the other enemy warships escape.

Such battles between the opposing capital ships were infrequent in the first two years of the war, and while battlecruisers were engaged, the big dreadnoughts and super dreadnoughts had yet to prove their investment. That was all to change at Jutland.

HMS *DREADNOUGHT* CAPTAINS (INCLUDING KNOWN DATES OF APPOINTMENT)

Captain Reginald H.S. Bacon – 2 July 1906
Captain Charles E. Madden – 12 August 1907–1 December 1908
Captain Charles Bartolomé – 1 December 1908–24 February 1909
Captain A. Gordon H.W. Moore – 1 December 1908–30 July 1909
Captain Herbert W. Richmond – 30 July 1909–4 April 1911
Captain Sydney R. Fremantle – 28 March 1911–17 December 1912
Captain Wilmot S. Nicholson – 17 December 1912–1 July 1914
Captain William J.S. Alderson – 1 July 1914–19 July 1916
Captain John W.L. McClintock – 19 July 1916–1 December 1916
Captain Arthur C.S. H. D'Aeth – 1 December 1916
Captain Thomas E. Wardle – January 1918–20 April 1918
Captain Maurice S. FitzMaurice – 20 April 1918–5 October 1918
Captain Robert H. Coppinger – 25 February 1919–31 March 1920

The Battle of Jutland

The Battle of Jutland was the high point of battleship warfare in history. On 31 May 1916, the German High Seas Fleet under Admiral Reinhard Scheer, plus heavy scouting forces commanded by Admiral Franz von Hipper, sailed out into the North Sea, intent on forcing a decisive combat with elements of the British Grand Fleet, such as Beatty's Battlecruiser Force. The German scouting force alone comprised 5 battlecruisers and 35 other vessels, while the main element totalled 22 dreadnoughts, super dreadnoughts or battlecruisers, as well as 37 other warships. Once the foray was detected, the entire British Grand Fleet was mobilised and set out to sail to intercept the German fleet. Some 24 of the 99 ships in this force were dreadnoughts, plus there were 52 ships in Beatty's battlecruiser formation, with 6 battlecruisers and 4 super dreadnoughts forming its big-gun element. The scene was set for the most bruising of naval encounters.

For some hours the two sides moved in a complex dance as they attempted to find and intercept one another, although the precise composition of the opposing forces was unclear to each side. Beatty's scouts spotted Hipper's force on the afternoon of 31 May, and at 3.48pm the battle commenced, with heavy fire at 16,500yd range. The opening stages of

LEFT The forward guns of HMS *Ajax*, their muzzles plugged with tampions to prevent damage to the bores from seawater.

the battle did not go to plan for Beatty. The battlecruiser *Indefatigable* was obliterated by shells from *Von der Tann*, the British ship torn apart in two explosions that killed all but two of her crew. *Derfflinger* inflicted a similar fate on the battlecruiser *Queen Mary*, although before her destruction *Queen Mary* had scored several very heavy hits on *Seydlitz*. Beatty pressed his attack, but then found himself facing the entire High Seas Fleet, forcing him to flee in a running battle that lasted two hours and saw strikes on both sides. Yet Scheer and Hipper were now being drawn into a direct clash with the Grand Fleet.

This clash came, much to the Scheer's shock, at 6.30pm, when Jellicoe's Grand Fleet began firing its first shells at the German ranks. Awe-inspiring firepower was unleashed, in which both fleets took hits and fatalities. During this clash, the British even managed to 'cross the German T', which prompted Scheer to disengage and attempt to withdraw, although he took his forces back into action around 7.00pm, attempting to take advantage of a perceived (but incorrect) split in the British fleet.

The two fleets broke apart shortly after, and although Jellicoe attempted to block the German escape, he failed to do so – an action that produced a storm of political and public controversy after the battle. When the final accounting was taken, the British had lost three battlecruisers (the two mentioned above plus *Invincible*, also destroyed following a magazine explosion), three cruisers and eight destroyers, plus 5,069 dead mariners. On the German side, the final tally was one battleship, *Lützow* (which sank *Invincible* but received 24 shell strikes, and was eventually scuttled), one battlecruiser, three cruisers and five destroyers, with 2,115 dead.

With full recognition of the human cost of the battle, Jutland was nevertheless an epic laboratory for educating the British about the

LEFT Admiral Reinhard Scheer, commander of the German High Seas Fleet during the Battle of Jutland in 1916. (LOC)

LEFT One of many tragedies of the Battle of Jutland – HMS *Indefatigible* burns and sinks after being hit by shells from the German battlecruiser *Von der Tann*.

CENTRE The super dreadnought *Erin*, equipped with 13.5in guns, was a war purchase addition to the Royal Navy, having originally been built for Turkey.

combat readiness of its Navy. Several key lessons emerged, some painfully, from the action. (The full Royal Navy account of the battle is given in this book in the Appendix.) There was the need for more effective scouting and reconnaissance procedures, and also for improvements in inter-ship wireless communications. There was a paramount need to improve gunnery, as it was felt that the Germans demonstrated a greater skill in fire control. The destruction of the three battlecruisers highlighted the most important lesson of all – the need for British warships to have adequate armour arrangements, to as much as possible prevent the catastrophic magazine detonations seen during the clash. The post-Jutland debates were complex, and remain so today, with a dispute still alive about the rights and wrongs of British warship design. Some of the official recommendations to emerge were collected as follows:

10. *Points particularly recommended for investigation:*

(a) *The position of magazines — whether they should not all be placed as low as possible in a ship, and on the centre line.*

(b) *The protection of magazines from shell fire and torpedoes. Observing that the penetration of one hot splinter to a magazine may be sufficient to cause explosion of the contents.*

(c) *The need of additional protection to roof plates, glacis, trunk of all turrets, and*

LEFT Shell damage inflicted on the forward superstructure of *Colossus* at Jutland. There were no fatalities, and only six men were injured.

particularly of 'Q' turret, since most hits occur on this central part of ships.

(d) The British design of turret, with sloping front and roof plates, increases the chance of penetration by shell at long range by providing a surface nearer the normal than if the front plates were vertical and the roof plates horizontal.

(e) The provision of a separate explosion trunk from all handling rooms to the upper deck, to provide some egress for gas pressures other than through the trunk and turret.

(f) The design of flash doors throughout

13.5" and 12" turrets appears to have been based only on the necessity of defeating back flame from the gun, which is small in volume and produces no gas pressure comparable with that of a shell burst or ignition of cordite in the turret. The numerous holes in gunhouse and working chamber floors and sides are a decided source of danger.

(g) The abolition of igniters permanently fitted to charges.

(h) The protection of charges by a light metal envelope capable of volatilisation on firing.

(i) The apparent immunity of German nitro-

ABOVE The *Orion-*
class battleship
Thunderer fired a total
of 37 13.5in rounds
during the Battle of
Jutland, which she
survived unscathed.

BELOW Not a
dreadnought, but the
badly damaged *Acasta-*
class destroyer HMS
Spitfire illustrates the
ferocity of the Jutland
fighting. *Spitfire* was
actually in a collision
with the German
dreadnought *Nassau*.

cellulose propellants from explosion by
shell fire, as compared with cordite.
(j) *The ready communication of explosion from
one magazine to another widely separated.*
(k) *The safety of nose-fuzes in common H.E.
shell.*
(l) *The stowage of shell in bins in gunhouses
and working chambers of turrets.*
(m) *The introduction of the Q.F. principle of
Breech Mechanism for all future guns.*
*David Beatty, letter to the Permanent
Secretary to the Board of Admiralty, Sir W.
Graham Greene, 14 July 1916*

All of these factors fed, to a greater or lesser
extent, into post-First World War battleship
design. Yet in some ways, even Jutland
demonstrated that the era of the dreadnought

and super dreadnought was already waning. There would always be a limit to how heavily a warship could be armoured before it became unwieldy. However, there was also the recognition that the vertical armour configuration of the big battleships had to change to give more deck protection from plunging long-range fire. It was this process of redesign, plus a gradual increase in the volume of secondary armament, that fed into the post-First World War era of the battleship, and the notion of the all-big-gun dreadnought and super dreadnought began to slip from use.

The end of the dreadnoughts

The end of the First World War was far from the end of Britain's battleship-building programme. Indeed, some of the greatest warships of the Royal Navy's history were launched during the 1920s, '30s and '40s, including the battlecruisers *Tiger*, *Repulse* and *Hood*, the five ships that composed the *King George V* class, and HMS *Vanguard*, the last battleship in history to be launched, in 1946.

Even as these ships were being developed and launched, the great dreadnoughts and super dreadnoughts were suffering the depredations of obsolescence. The 1920s was a particularly intense time for the scrapping of dreadnought ships. *Dreadnought* herself went to the scrapper's yard in 1921, as did *Bellerophon*, *Superb*, *St Vincent* and *Hercules*. The following year they were joined by *Collingwood*, *Neptune*, *Agincourt*, *Conqueror* and *Orion*. The rate of attrition was rapid, and by 1928 all the British dreadnoughts were gone, plus eight of the super dreadnoughts. Of the remaining super dreadnoughts, their more advanced firepower and steady modifications ensured that some lasted through the inter-war years and even served during the Second World War. This was especially the case with the *Queen Elizabeth*- and *Royal Sovereign*-class vessels. Of those, *Barham* and *Royal Oak* did not survive the war, for reasons already outlined above, while the others toughed it out through the conflict years, despite seeing frequent action. HMS *Warspite*, for example, served in Atlantic, European, Mediterranean, and Indian Ocean theatres between 1939 and 1945, surviving air attacks, mines, shellfire and even strikes by an

ABOVE The battlecruiser HMS *Tiger* was hit 14 times during the Battle of Jutland. Here we see the crushing damage inflicted on one of her barbettes. Ten of her crew members were killed during the action.

BELOW This brooding photograph shows the last moments of HMS *Queen Mary*, destroyed after a magazine explosion at the Battle of Jutland.

RIGHT An early photograph of the USS *Texas*, still showing the two large lattice masts which were subsequently replaced by a more modern tripod mast during modernisation in 1925–6. *(US Navy)*

USS *TEXAS*

The USS *Texas* was a *New York*-class battleship, laid down on 17 April 1911, launched on 18 May 1912 and commissioned on 12 March 1914. Several points stand out about *Texas*. First is her longevity. *Texas* is today the only surviving dreadnought battleship, displayed and preserved as a museum ship at the San Jacinto Battleground State Historic Park near Houston, Texas. *Texas* served fully in both world wars before her decommissioning in 1948, her relevance in the Second World War aided by a major refit in 1925–26, another in 1942, plus numerous other modifications in the 1930s and 1940s that kept the ship safe from obsolescence.

As built, the warship had a displacement of 27,000 long tons and was armed with

10 × 14in guns, 21 × 5in guns and 10 smaller-calibre weapons. Her maximum speed was 21 knots and range 7,060 miles. By 1945, the ship was displacing 32,000 long tons and in addition to her unchanged 14in guns had just 6 × 5in guns but 10 × 3in, 10 × quad 40mm, and 44 × 20mm guns. Her fire-control systems had also been massively upgraded, to include the radar systems. It was because of such changes that *Texas* had an operational career that included convoy escort in both world wars, but important shore bombardment roles in both Operations *Torch* and *Overlord* during the Second World War. It is satisfying that when so many ships went to the scrapyard just after the war, *Texas* was saved for posterity.

RIGHT A starboard view of *Texas* as she sits today, docked in the Houston Ship Channel as a museum ship. *(Frank H. Bruecker)*

ABOVE USS *Texas* passes through the Gatun Locks in the Panama Canal in 1937. By this time *Texas* had the very latest in fire-control systems; here we can see a large rangefinder atop the bridge. *(US Navy)*

BELOW The business end of USS *Texas* – the battleship had 10 × 14in guns as main armament. After her 1942 refit, she also boasted more than 70 anti-aircraft guns. *(Frank H. Bruecker)*

early German guided missile (the Fritz X), off the coast of Italy in 1943.

Such service, however, could not save any of the super dreadnoughts from scrapping. Almost all the super dreadnoughts were decommissioned and broken up during the second half of the 1940s, the exception being *Canada*, which had been returned to Chile in 1920 and defied scrapping until 1959. Today, all that remains of the dreadnought era is the battleship USS *Texas*, an important reminder of an age when battleships were ascendant.

ABOVE *Dreadnought*'s gunners proudly display a shredded target after gunnery trials. *(NMRN)*

BELOW A US Division of Naval Intelligence book explains the identifying characteristics of the *Royal Sovereign* class.

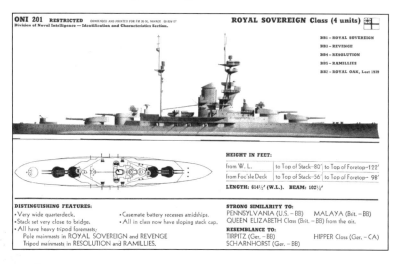

ONI 201 RESTRICTED CONDENSED AND PRINTED FM 30-50, NAVAEX 50-REV-57
Division of Naval Intelligence — Identification and Characteristics Section.

ROYAL SOVEREIGN Class (4 units)

BB1 – ROYAL SOVEREIGN
BB3 – REVENGE
BB4 – RESOLUTION
BB5 – RAMILLIES
BB2 – ROYAL OAK, Lost 1939

HEIGHT IN FEET:

from W. L.	to Top of Stack–80'	to Top of Foretop–122'
from Foc'sle Deck	to Top of Stack–56'	to Top of Foretop– 98'

LENGTH: 614½' (W.L.). BEAM: 102½'

DISTINGUISHING FEATURES:
• Very wide quarterdeck.
• Stack set very close to bridge.
• All have heavy tripod foremasts;
  Pole mainmasts in ROYAL SOVEREIGN and REVENGE
  Tripod mainmasts in RESOLUTION and RAMILLIES.
• Casemate battery recesses amidships.
• All in class now have sloping stack cap.

STRONG SIMILARITY TO:
PENNSYLVANIA (U.S. – BB)   MALAYA (Brit. – BB)
QUEEN ELIZABETH Class (Brit. – BB) from the air.

RESEMBLANCE TO:
TIRPITZ (Ger. – BB)   HIPPER Class (Ger. – CA)
SCHARNHORST (Ger. – BB)

Chapter Seven

The restoration of HMS *Caroline*

HMS *Caroline* is a remarkable piece of history. The last survivor of the Battle of Jutland, this ship has been brought to life for the public once again through a dedicated restoration effort in the Alexandra Graving Dock in Belfast.

OPPOSITE *Caroline* as she stands today at Alexandra Graving Dock in Belfast, just a few hundred yards from the location where *Titanic* was constructed. *(DUOM0803)*

This book has been focused principally on the British dreadnoughts and super dreadnoughts; those mighty vessels that were the epitome of Royal Navy power projection in the first half of the 20th century. Yet while in their prime they must have once cast an aura of permanence and longevity, as we have seen, their time on the world stage was all too brief. By 1945, the era of the battleship in general was over, and many of the dreadnoughts had already been scrapped, the cutter's lance burning through gun barrels that once hurled huge shells across miles of ocean. Only one dreadnought survives today – the USS *Texas*, anchored appropriately in Houston, Texas.

Yet incredibly, there is a survivor from the Battle of Jutland itself. HMS *Caroline*, a C-class light cruiser, was laid down in 1914 but in one form or another survived as functioning MOD property until 2011. Since then, she has been deservedly saved from demolition, and is now undergoing a painstaking restoration that will bring this important warship to life for the general public.

The *Caroline*-class cruisers

The focus of this book on dreadnought-sized vessels can distract us from the fact that battleships were just one strata of warship within a huge Royal Navy. Notwithstanding the many battlecruisers launched conterminously with the dreadnoughts, there were also dozens of cruisers, light cruisers, destroyers, torpedo boats and other vessels launched and commissioned within the space of a couple of decades. During the First World War, the British Grand Fleet consisted of about 160 vessels, but only between 35 and 40 of these were capital warships.

So where did HMS *Caroline* fit into this spectrum of floating firepower? *Caroline* was the lead ship of a six-ship class, consisting of *Caroline*, *Carysfort*, *Cleopatra*, *Comus*, *Conquest* and *Cordelia*. (Note, however, that sometimes this class is referred to as the *Comus* class.) In turn, the *Caroline* class was one of seven classes that composed the C class of light cruiser, 28 ships in total. These classes were *Caroline*, *Calliope*, *Cambrian*, *Centaur*, *Caledon*, *Ceres* and *Carlisle*, and were ordered in the 1913–17 programmes of shipbuilding.

Although ships like *Caroline* are typically referred to as 'light cruisers', their full title was 'light armoured cruisers'. With respectable

LEFT A postcard depicts *Caroline* in her 1917 configuration. She has just a single tripod mast forward, and the rear superstructure features 6in and 4in guns.

speed, armour and firepower, these ships were intended to fulfil a wide variety of roles unsuited to the large capital vessels, including scouting, escorting merchant vessels and fleet support. The specifications of *Caroline* provide us with a good insight into the C class in general.

Caroline was ordered within the 1913 programme, and was to be constructed by the Cammell Laird shipbuilder at Birkenhead. The ship was laid down on 28 January 1914 and launched almost exactly eight months later, on 29 September. Her overall length was 446ft, with a beam of 41.5ft and a maximum draught of 16ft. Displacement, in loaded state, was 4,219 tons. For propulsion, *Caroline* was powered by four-shaft Parsons turbines generating 40,000shp, giving a maximum speed of 28.5 knots. Note, however, that to its detriment *Caroline* did not have geared turbines, a fact that reduced her performance at lower speeds. Later ships of the C class were supplied with the geared powerplant.

In terms of armament, as-built *Caroline* had two BL 6in/45 Mk XII guns, both set aft in single mounts, plus eight QF 4in/45 Mk V guns (two forward, three on each beam), one 6-pdr gun and four 21in torpedo tubes. The decision to

CENTRE The Parsons turbines on *Caroline* generated 40,000shp and drove four shafts. This image shows the turbines in their current state. *(NMRN)*

RIGHT The crew of *Caroline* gather around a newspaper, which based on the 'John Bull' title is obviously stirring stuff. *(NMRN)*

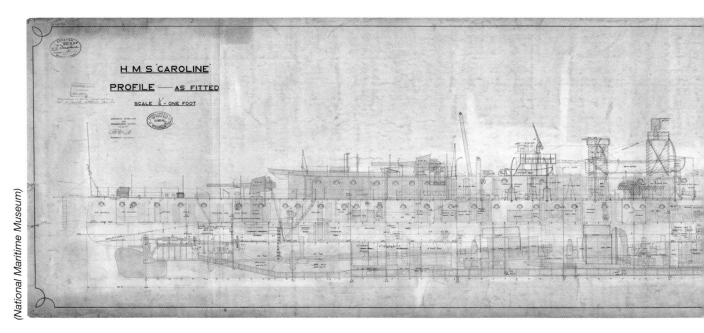

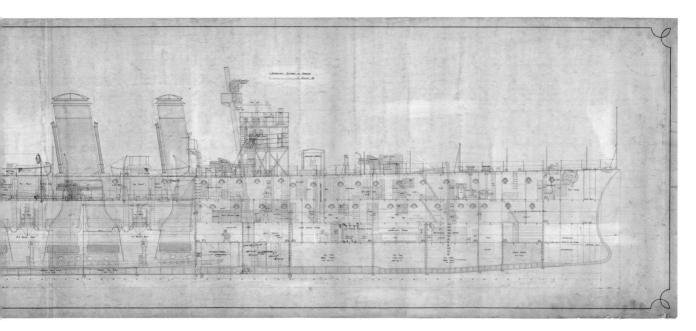

mount both 6in guns aft was taken to make fire-control easier, and to give the main armament a better platform in rough seas.

Caroline's original armament configuration, and indeed that of many of those in the C class, was changed significantly between 1914 and 1918, based on combat feedback and comparison with German armament set-ups. The 4in guns forward were replaced in 1916 by another 6in single, and a 4in HA gun for anti-aircraft work replaced the 3-pdr. Gradually all 4in guns were removed and replaced with 4in HA weapons, and a fourth 6in gun was mounted on a platform abaft the funnels. Experience showed that the heavier 6in guns had a superior tactical performance to the 4in weapons, hence the gravitation in that direction.

Given the type of ship it was, Caroline's armour was necessarily light when compared to the sonorous walls of the dreadnoughts.

OPPOSITE AND RIGHT One of the most impressive sections of *Caroline* is the emergency steering gear down in the lower aft hull. If the standard steering gear was knocked out, crew members could manually move the rudder via the bank of wooden ship's wheels, geared directly to the rudder. Directional information was given on an overhead dial, which was moved by a system of geared linkages, also seen in the steering room.

The belt armour was just 3–1in while the deck armour was 1in. Clearly it would be a bad day if a C-class cruiser were hit by a 12in shell.

Caroline's history

RIGHT **One of the few original signs left on *Caroline*, explaining where important items such as rifles and, apparently, a side drum can be found.**

RIGHT **One of the dozens of hatches around *Caroline*, here with the hatch lid in its locked-up position, plus an anti-fall grille in place.**

By the time *Caroline* was commissioned into service on 4 December 1914, the First World War was already under way, so the ship went straight into wartime operations. This initially meant conducting patrols in the North Sea and also forming part of convoy screens to protect vulnerable merchant ships against the depredations of German U-boats and surface vessels. *Caroline* performed these duties without firing a shot in anger. Indeed, its guns might have stayed silent for the entire war had not it been involved in the greatest naval surface engagement in history, the Battle of Jutland on 31 May–1 June 1916. An urgent steering gear repair meant that *Caroline* didn't leave Scapa Flow to join the Grand Fleet until the evening of 30 May, after which she took up position in the fleet-screening force, one of a number of ships trying to spot the German High Seas Fleet, while acting as a protective shield to the major warships. At around 6.07pm on 31 May, *Caroline* was drawn into the growing shooting battle, witnessing the battlecruiser *Invincible* blowing up at 6.31pm. Then at 7.30pm *Caroline* added its firepower to the clash: at a range of 9,200yd, *Caroline* fired three 6in and four 9in rounds at a German destroyer, before disengaging. Then, at 9.00pm, *Caroline* and the light cruiser *Royalist* came into contact with the main German battleline, including the dreadnought *Nassau*. After getting clearance to fire from commander of the 2nd Battle Squadron, Admiral Sir Martyn Jerram, both ships launched torpedoes towards the enemy, without result, before retreating under the resultant enemy fire. (One heavy German shell actually passed between the wireless deck and the upper deck.) *Caroline* then returned to Scapa Flow on 2 June.

ABOVE During her days serving the Ulster Division, *Caroline* had a small-bore rifle range set along this starboard deck section. *(Jef Maytom)*

LEFT At the forward end of the ship, the anchor chain was found stored (and rusting) in the storage compartments closed with the wooden planking. *(Jef Maytom)*

BELOW LEFT AND BELOW *Caroline*'s bridge and navigating platform. Reconstruction has revealed the brass framework that insulated the bridge instruments from electromagnetic interference. *(Jef Maytom)*

RIGHT One of the ship's heads. It was in such a space that original sections of paintwork were discovered.
(Jef Maytom)

FAR RIGHT A steering column connection. One runs down each side of the ship.
(Jef Maytom)

FAR RIGHT One of the many storerooms and spaces in *Caroline*, which over the years have served purposes ranging from mess decks to training rooms and offices.
(Jef Maytom)

BELOW Two of the tripod mast legs running down beneath the main deck.
(Jef Maytom)

One other notable event in *Caroline*'s wartime career was the fitting of a flying-off platform in 1918. This platform, mounted over the forward 6in gun, allowed a Sopwith 2F.1 'Camel' single-seat scout aircraft to fly from the ship on reconnaissance duties. The modification was something of an unsuccessful experiment. Launching the aircraft required that *Caroline* turn into the wind, something not always practical under operational circumstances, plus there was no means to bring the aircraft back on board – it either had to ditch and the pilot be rescued, or, more commonly, the aircraft would land on shore and be brought back to the ship on a supply vessel.

1918–45

In 1917 and 1918, *Caroline* spent much of her time in dock for refits and repairs, although she also participated in blockade actions against the weakening Germany. One of the most dramatic, and horrifying, incidents witnessed by *Caroline*'s crew was the destruction of HMS *Vanguard* on 9 July 1918 at Scapa Flow, the *St Vincent*-class dreadnought blown apart by an accidental magazine detonation.

The war ended in November 1918, at which point *Caroline*'s status was care and maintenance, but in June 1919 she was recommissioned for the East Indies station. She sailed for the duty on 29 March from Pembroke Dock, reaching the station around Christmas time after visiting Malta, British Somaliland (after traversing the Suez Canal), Aden, Bombay, Colombo and finally Calcutta.

In November 1921, *Caroline* began the journey to Britain after her foreign service. This time it did seem that the writing was on the wall for the ship, and from January 1922 until 1924 she sat at Portsmouth, awaiting the scrapping order. Unlike so many of her contemporaries,

however, that order never came. She was saved by the formation of the Ulster Division of the Royal Naval Volunteer Reserve; *Caroline* was chosen to be the division's drill ship in Belfast. Having been towed to Belfast, the ship needed extensive modification to facilitate her new static role. The adaptation process, performed by Harland and Wolff, included:

■ A deckhouse built over the aft upper deck
■ Removal of the ship's boilers (the turbines were left in place)

■ Conversion of numerous rooms into instruction spaces and workshops.

Eventually anchored in the Musgrave Channel, the modified *Caroline* began its busy life as a training ship. The division instructed in a variety of skills aboard the ship, including torpedo handling, gunnery, wireless communications, small-arms handling (a small-bore rifle range was installed along the starboard side of the ship) and various other general aspects of naval life. At its high

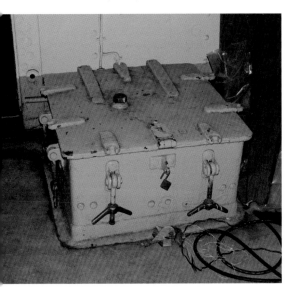

RIGHT The hatch leading down into the emergency steering room.

FAR RIGHT A hole through *Caroline*'s hull shows the depth of the armour thickness – 3–1in on the belt.

BELOW Electrical junction boxes set in the drill hall. During restoration the ship has required some rewiring to comply with current safety regulations.

BELOW RIGHT Signal lighting is often seen over hatches leading down to important spaces, such as shell rooms and engine rooms.

point during this period, more than 350 men frequented the warship at any one time.

The outbreak of the Second World War in 1939 changed *Caroline*'s status. The drafting of the Ulster Division sailors meant that the Ulster Division of the RNR temporarily ceased to exist, so *Caroline* was taken back into Royal Navy service, acting as a base ship for trawlers and other light craft, providing signal and cypher facilities, and also training sailors and merchant seamen in gunnery techniques.

1946–2011

Once the war ended in 1945, *Caroline* was able to go back to her previous role with the Ulster Division RNR, a function that she would perform for the next 60 years. *Caroline* was returned to the Harland and Wolff yard for additional modification, including the fitting of new funnels, and the ship also underwent

some modernisation in the 1950s. It is worth remembering, however, that despite a series of structural and purpose modifications since the 1920s, *Caroline* still retained many original spaces, including the bridge, tripod mast, foretop, main galley, wardroom, main galley, sick bay, shower rooms and many other spaces. The existence of this original layout would be of great assistance to the ship's future restoration.

As the years passed, *Caroline* had direct experience of the 'Troubles' that flared up in earnest in Northern Ireland during the 1960s and 1970s. In September 1971, a sniper fired a bullet through one of the legs of the ship's tripod mast. More seriously, in August 1972 a bomb laid by the Irish Republican Army (IRA) detonated in a nearby shed used by the Gunnery School on Milewater Wharf, where *Caroline* was berthed. Thankfully nobody was

ABOVE AND LEFT
Fuseboxes and
electrical junctions.
Restoration revealed
that significant
amounts of *Caroline*'s
original material and
engineering structures
continued to exist.

ABOVE One of the officers' cabins, complete with an original electric bar fire boxed on the wall.

ABOVE RIGHT A shower room – note the header tank and valve at the top of the picture. Note also the slight dent in the hull frame on the left, the damage left when a Royal Navy minesweeper struck *Caroline*.

killed or wounded, although the ship did suffer some minor blast damage.

Caroline dutifully served as a reserve unit until 2009, although during the 1990s there had been some discussion about the Imperial War Museum (IWM) taking her over as an exhibit ship at Hartlepool. In December 2009, however, the ship was decommissioned as a reserve unit and the ship herself was decommissioned on 31 March 2011. Not wishing to see this historic vessel go to ruin, the National Museum of the Royal Navy (NMRN) took over her care, although the long-term future remained uncertain.

Restoration

The restoration of HMS *Caroline* is a story of vision and determination, plus the successful negotiation of the acres of paperwork that need completing for a viable restoration project. In 2011–12 various proposals about *Caroline* were in discussion, including restoring the entire ship back to a facsimile of its original configuration, and also moving the ship to Portsmouth. In October 2012, however, the Northern Ireland government announced that *Caroline* would stay in Belfast, integrated as it was into the Belfast community, and over the next two years the National Heritage Memorial Fund and the Heritage Lottery Fund provided the primary means – funding of £12 million – to convert the vessel into a museum ship for the general public.

At the outset there were challenges for both restoration but also interpretation. *Caroline* had been in service for a century, and had undergone a huge amount of physical change over that time, so decisions had to be made about what elements to preserve, and what aspects needed to be returned to an earlier phase. Jonathan Porter, the project manager on the *Caroline* restoration, explained some of the objectives in an interview with the author:

There were two key considerations. We obviously had to safeguard and maintain the historical significance of the ship, and we also had to do an interpretation package which made telling the story of the ship interesting and informative. So it was really a balance between both of those. An example would be that certain areas of the ship may have historical timbers dating back to when she was constructed in 1914 – you'd have to worship those timbers – whereas the bit nailed to the wall right beside them was due for the skip. We spent a huge amount of time doing a full assessment of what was on board, whether it was significant from an historical point of view, and what sort of stories could be told. It was really that sort of forensic analysis at the outset that informed the plan of how we were going to do the interpretation package. That led the team to the position that rather than take the whole ship back to its configuration at the Battle of Jutland, it was important to really tell the story of the ship throughout the years. … The story was bigger than 1914.

A critical element in making all the right decisions about the restoration was to understand exactly how *Caroline* had appeared at various stages of her history. An Interpretation Team, consisting of Jef Maytom (Interpretive Planner & Content Development Director) working in partnership with Erich Kadow (Interpretive Planner & Design Director) and a broader team, conducted a thorough interpretative archaeological investigation of the ship, going back to the moment the ship was built and running the story through to the present day. Jonathan Porter here explains the approach and some of the fortunate finds:

We were quite lucky because we have quite a lot of the plans dating right back to when she was constructed. Then there were obviously quite a lot of fill-ins throughout the decades – adding bits and taking bits off, mending bits, etc. – so they used those and any research material they could get to do a forensic analysis of what was where and when. … That whole exercise put the story together on how she was altered and amended for her various roles throughout the decades, right down to the paint analysis. … They were able to get a chunk of paint from behind the toilets on the fo'c'sle deck, where people obviously couldn't be bothered to scrape it off. They did a chemical cross-section through the paint, and they were able to tell every colour the ship was painted from the day she was constructed to today. From their point of view that was an incredible find,

ABOVE Another view of the starboard main deck, where the RNR used to have their small-bore rifle range.

ABOVE LEFT A starboard side corridor. The restoration team has diligently had to remove all traces of asbestos from any pipework running through the ship.

because obviously colour photography only really came in properly in the 1950s, so none of us knew what colour the ship had really been back in the day. So they were able to tell that in 1922, when she went to the East Indies, she had been painted in a sort of white and primrose yellow colour scheme.

BELOW A view from the forecastle deck down to the drill hall entrance at the far end, a deck below.

ABOVE LEFT AND ABOVE Two views of the forecastle deck and the associated fittings, including air vent pipes, inspection hatches, bow cables and anchor chains.

LEFT AND BELOW *Caroline*'s forecastle deck looking down to the bridge structure and the foretop on the tripod mast. *Caroline*'s deck guns are long gone, and replica versions have been installed since this photograph was taken.

The paint find was indeed an exciting moment in the project, although perhaps the depth of the excitement is not immediately apparent to those who do not immerse their lives in such matters. Jef Maytom, in interview for a Royal Navy article, remarked: 'This finding rewrites the rule book for historians specialising in naval and maritime history. It is the equivalent of a palaeontologist being able to finally prove that dinosaurs were a specific colour or had feathers.'

Once armed with detailed information about the ship's physical evolution, the restoration team could then go about deciding how to present the ship's timeline to the public through its physical space. Although the team had debated taking the ship back to her 1916 configuration, in the end it was felt that the long history of the ship needed representing in a broader fashion. Jonathan Porter here explains the overarching historical layout of the restored ship, as conceived at the time of writing in late 2015:

> In terms of the arrangement, the after end on the upper deck is basically the ship nearly as it was at the Battle of Jutland, so the rear third is the officers' cabins, wardroom, etc. – this all lends itself to that period. As you go forward through the ship, the next section lends itself more to the time she was in the East Indies. Then we have the drill hall, which we'll use as the audio-visual exhibition space about the Battle of Jutland. We'll also have the historic engine rooms; we'll install a gantry around those and restore them to as they were originally installed – we'll tell the story of the Parsons turbines. As you go forward the ship essentially gets younger – you move through the decades. At the very forward end of the ship where you have the junior rates' mess, where the junior rates would have eaten and slept, we were

ABOVE AND BELOW
The ship's galley, with ovens and grill plate. Note the hot water taps running off the stoves.

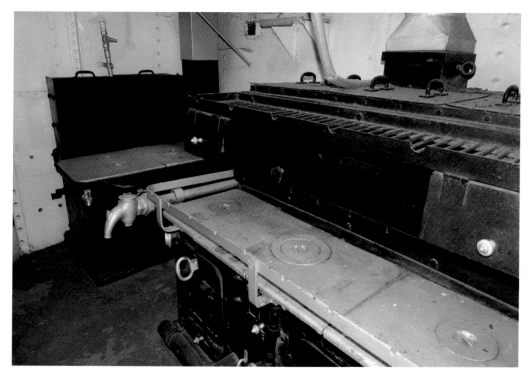

ABOVE The forward magazine room, with wooden blocks for the 6in shells.

originally going to keep it as a 1970s social club, but then the decision was taken to turn it into part of the café area, but set-dressed as a junior rates' mess.

Needless to say, the restoration effort surrounding this work has been intensive. Warships are tough environments to work in, claustrophobic, dark and dangerous. A key priority for the restoration, for example, has been the removal of asbestos from the ship. In times past asbestos was used heavily in ship construction as a heat-protecting and insulating material, liberally applied to engines, boilers and around the steam pipes that laced their way through the ship. Given the carcinogenic properties of asbestos (although only in its fragmented, broken state, when its dust can be inhaled), all traces of the material will be removed before the first member of the public sets foot aboard.

The restoration manager, Billy Hughes, also had to focus efforts on preserving the time-worn ship from elemental damage. In 2010, while the ship was still under MOD control, the severe cold weather during the winter months resulted in pipework and radiators bursting, leading to localised flooding that potentially threatened to sink the ship. Captain John Rees, chief of staff at the Portsmouth-based National Museum of the Royal Navy and senior responsible officer for HMS *Caroline*, said in an interview for the *News Letter* in 2013: 'Thanks to the vigilance and quick thinking of Billy Hughes, the flood water was pumped out of the engine rooms just in time. But we are confident that the measures we are taking now will protect the vessel from possible further damage should the temperatures fall below zero.'

The team also had to remove deck timbers to enhance waterproofing, and a detailed survey of the hull was undertaken to check its integrity, which still seems essentially sound even though

RIGHT *Caroline*'s forward mess deck (hammock hooks can still be spotted on some beams), with two hawse pipes running through.

it has spent more than a century in saltwater. In 2010 the ship also went through inclining tests, with up to 20 tonnes of weights lifted on board by cranes to check that the ship met IMO (International Maritime Organization) criteria for a ship under severe wind and weather conditions.

The author was walked through the ship during the writing of this book, and some of the photographs from that visit are displayed in this chapter. To those unused to warships, the primary sensation below decks is, at first, one of slight disorientation, as you attempt to get your bearings through a labyrinth of corridors, passages, hatches, ladders, steps and rooms. *Caroline* is no exception, despite being far smaller than the huge dreadnoughts and super dreadnoughts that form the primary focus of this book. Jonathan Porter also commented on the ship's layout:

The ship doesn't look that big from the outside – she's fairly slender – but what I couldn't get over was the sheer amount of compartmentation. The sheer number of rooms on board was unbelievable – they run into their hundreds. The ship was able to accommodate 250 men once she was fully laden, including Marines. I was impressed by the sheer volume and the best use of space. ... The junior rates' mess was just laid out with bench seats, and the tables

and benches were simply folded down at night and hammocks were slung up, and the people basically just slept where they ate earlier in the day. You sort of get a sense of how the people would have lived on board and shared the spaces.

Caroline is indeed a remarkable piece of history. The faithfulness of the restoration means that visitors will truly be able to absorb the life of a Jutland-era warship at close quarters, from the engineers down in the engine room to the spotters swaying high up in the mainmast.

ABOVE The forward section of the ship, at the point where the bow plates join together.

LEFT A stern view of *Caroline*, clearly showing the large post-First World War cabin section added to the after deck area when the ship was transferred to the RNR. In December 2015 this cabin was removed to protect the materiality of the ship. (NMRN)

Appendix

Sir John Jellicoe's Report on the Battle of Jutland, 31 May–1 June 1916

24 June, 1916

Sir,

Be pleased to inform the Lords Commissioners of the Admiralty that the German High Sea Fleet was brought to action on May 31, 1916, to the westward of the Jutland Bank, off the coast of Denmark.

The ships of the Grand Fleet, in pursuance of the general policy of periodical sweeps through the North Sea, had left its bases on the previous day, in accordance with instructions issued by me.

In the early afternoon of Wednesday, May 31st, the 1st and 2nd Battle-cruiser Squadrons, 1st, 2nd and 3rd Lightcruiser Squadrons and destroyers from the 1st, 9th, 10th and 13th Flotillas, supported by the 5th Battle Squadron, were, in accordance with my directions, scouting to the southward of the Battle Fleet, which was accompanied by the 3rd Battlecruiser Squadron, 1st and 2nd Cruiser Squadrons, 4th Lightcruiser Squadron, 4th, 11th and 12th Flotillas.

The junction of the Battle Fleet with the scouting force after the enemy had been sighted was delayed owing to the southerly course steered by our advanced force during the first hour after commencing their action with the enemy battle-cruisers. This was, of course, unavoidable, as had our battle-cruisers not followed the enemy to the southward the main fleets would never have been in contact.

The Battle-cruiser Fleet, gallantly led by Vice-Admiral Sir David Beatty, and admirably supported by the ships of the Fifth Battle Squadron under Rear-Admiral Hugh Evan-Thomas, fought an action under, at times, disadvantageous conditions, especially, in regard to light, in a manner that was in keeping with the best traditions of the service.

On receipt of the information that the enemy had been sighted, the British Battle Fleet, with its accompanying cruiser and destroyer force, proceeded at full speed on a S.E. by S. course to close the Battle-cruiser Fleet.

During the two hours that elapsed before the arrival of the Battle Fleet on the scene the steaming qualities of the older battleships were severely tested. Great credit is due to the engine-room departments for the manner in which they, as always, responded to the call, the whole Fleet maintaining a speed in excess of the trial speeds of some of the older vessels.

The Third Battle-cruiser Squadron, which was in advance of the Battle Fleet, was ordered to reinforce Sir David Beatty. At 5.30 p.m. this squadron observed flashes of gunfire and heard the sound of guns to the southwestward.

Rear-Admiral Hood sent the *Chester* to investigate, and this ship engaged three or four enemy light-cruisers at about 5.45 p.m. The engagement lasted for about twenty minutes, during which period Captain Lawson handled his vessel with great skill against heavy odds, and, although the ship suffered considerably in casualties, her fighting and steaming qualities were unimpaired, and at about 6.05 p.m. she rejoined the Third Battle-cruiser Squadron.

The Third Battle-cruiser Squadron had turned to the northwestward, and at 6.10 p.m. sighted our battle-cruisers, the squadron taking station ahead of the *Lion* at 6.21 p.m. in accordance with the orders of the Vice-Admiral Commanding Battle-cruiser Fleet.

Meanwhile, at 5.45 p.m., the report of guns had become audible to me, and at 5.55 p.m. flashes were visible from ahead round to the starboard beam, although in the mist no ships could be distinguished, and the position of the enemy's battle fleet could not be determined. The difference in estimated position by 'reckoning' between *Iron Duke* and *Lion*, which was inevitable under the circumstances, added to the uncertainty of the general situation.

Shortly after 5.55 p.m. some of the cruisers ahead were seen to be in action, and reports received show that *Defence*, flagship, and *Warrior*, of the First Cruiser Squadron, engaged an enemy light-cruiser at this time. She was subsequently observed to sink.

At 6 p.m. *Canterbury*, which ship was in company with the Third Battle-cruiser Squadron, had engaged enemy light-cruisers which were firing heavily on the torpedo-boat destroyers *Shark*, *Acasta* and *Christopher*; as a result of this engagement the *Shark* was sunk.

At 6 p.m. vessels, afterwards seen to be our battlecruisers, were sighted by *Marlborough* bearing before the starboard beam of the battle fleet.

At the same time the Vice-Admiral Commanding Battle-cruiser Fleet, reported to me the position of the enemy battle-cruisers, and at 6.14 p.m. reported the position of the enemy battle fleet.

At this period, when the battle fleet was meeting the battlecruisers and the Fifth Battle Squadron, great care was necessary to insure that our own ships were not mistaken for enemy vessels.

I formed the battle fleet in line of battle on receipt of Sir David Beatty's report, and during deployment the fleets became engaged. Sir David Beatty had meanwhile formed the battle-cruisers ahead of the battle fleet.

At 6.16 p.m. *Defence* and *Warrior* were observed passing down between the British and German Battle Fleets under a very heavy fire. *Defence* disappeared, and *Warrior* passed to the rear disabled.

It is probable that Sir Robert Arbuthnot, during his engagement with the enemy's light-cruisers and in his desire to complete their destruction, was not aware of the approach of the enemy's heavy ships, owing to the mist, until he found himself in close proximity to the main fleet, and before he could withdraw his ships they were caught under a heavy fire and disabled.

It is not known when *Black Prince*, of the same squadron, was sunk, but a wireless signal was received from her between 8 and 9 p.m.

The First Battle Squadron became engaged during deployment, the Vice-Admiral opening fire at 6.17 p.m. on a battleship of the *Kaiser* class. The other Battle Squadrons, which had previously been firing at an enemy light-cruiser, opened fire at 6.30 p.m. on battleships of the *Koenig* class.

At 6.06 p.m. the Rear-Admiral Commanding Fifth Battle Squadron, then in company with the battle-cruisers, had sighted the starboard wing division of the battle fleet on the port bow of *Barham*, and the first intention of Rear-Admiral Evan-Thomas was to form ahead of the remainder of the battle fleet, but on realizing the direction of deployment he was compelled to form astern, a manoeuvre which was well executed by the squadron under a heavy fire from the enemy battle fleet.

An accident to *Warspite*'s steering gear caused her helm to become jammed temporarily and took the ship in the direction of the enemy's line, during which time she was hit several times. Clever handling enabled Captain Edward M. Phillpotts to extricate his ship from a somewhat awkward situation.

Owing principally to the mist, but partly to the smoke, it was possible to see only a few ships at a time in the enemy's battle line. Towards the van only some four or five ships were ever visible at once. More could be seen from the rear squadron, but never more than eight to twelve.

The action between the battle fleets lasted intermittently from 6.17 p.m. to 8.20 p.m. at ranges between 9,000 and 12,000 yards, during which time the British Fleet made alterations of course from S.E. by E. to W. in the endeavour to close.

The enemy constantly turned away and opened the range under cover of destroyer attacks and smoke screens as the effect of the British fire was felt, and the alterations of course had the effect of bringing the British Fleet (which commenced the action in a position of advantage on the bow of the enemy) to a quarterly bearing from the enemy battle line, but at the same time placed us between the enemy and his bases.

At 6.55 p.m. *Iron Duke* passed the wreck of *Invincible*, with *Badger* standing by.

During the somewhat brief periods that the

ships of the High Sea Fleet were visible through the mist, the heavy and effective fire kept up by the battleships and battle-cruisers of the Grand Fleet caused me much satisfaction, and the enemy vessels were seen to be constantly hit, some being observed to haul out of the line and at least one to sink.

The enemy's return fire at this period was not effective, and the damage caused to our ships was insignificant.

As was anticipated, the German Fleet appeared to rely very much on torpedo attacks, which were favoured by the low visibility and by the fact that we had arrived in the position of a 'following' or 'chasing' fleet.

A large number of torpedoes were apparently fired, but only one took effect (on *Marlborough*), and even in this case the ship was able to remain in the line and to continue the action. The enemy's efforts to keep out of effective gun range were aided by the weather conditions, which were ideal for the purpose. Two separate destroyer attacks were made by the enemy.

The First Battle Squadron, under Vice-Admiral Sir Cecil Burney, came into action at 6.17 p.m. with the enemy's Third Battle Squadron, at a range of about 11,000 yards, and administered severe punishment, both to the battleships and to the battle-cruisers and light-cruisers, which were also engaged.

The fire of *Marlborough* (Captain George P. Ross) was particularly rapid and effective. This ship commenced at 6.17 p.m. by firing seven salvoes at a ship of the *Kaiser* class, then engaged a cruiser, and again a battleship, and at 6.54 she was hit by a torpedo and took up a considerable list to starboard, but reopened at 7.03 p.m. at a cruiser and at 7.12 p.m. fired fourteen rapid salvoes at a ship of the *Koenig* class, hitting her frequently until she turned out of the line.

The manner in which this effective fire was kept up in spite of the disadvantages due to the injury caused by the torpedo was most creditable to the ship and a very fine example to the squadron.

The range decreased during the course of the action to 9,000 yards. The First Battle Squadron received more of the enemy's return fire than the remainder of the battle fleet, with the exception of the Fifth Battle Squadron.

Colossus was hit but was not seriously damaged, and other ships were straddled with fair frequency.

In the Fourth Battle Squadron – in which squadron my flagship *Iron Duke* was placed – Vice-Admiral Sir Doveton Sturdee leading one of the divisions – the enemy engaged was the squadron consisting of *Koenig* and *Kaiser* class and some of the battle-cruisers, as well as disabled cruisers and light-cruisers.

The mist rendered range-taking a difficult matter, but the fire of the squadron was effective. *Iron Duke*, having previously fired at a light-cruiser between the lines, opened fire at 6.30 p.m. on a battleship of the *Koenig* class at a range of 12,000 yards. The latter was very quickly straddled, and hitting commenced at the second salvo and only ceased when the target ship turned away.

The rapidity with which hitting was established was most creditable to the excellent gunnery organization of the flagship.

The fire of other ships of the squadron was principally directed at enemy battle-cruisers and cruisers as they appeared out of the mist. Hits were observed to take effect on several ships.

The ships of the Second Battle Squadron, under Vice-Admiral Sir Thomas Jerram, were in action with vessels of the *Kaiser* or *Koenig* classes between 6.30 and 7.20 p.m., and fired also at an enemy battle-cruiser which had dropped back apparently severely damaged.

During the action between the battle fleets the Second Cruiser Squadron, ably commanded by Rear-Admiral Herbert L. Heath, with the addition of *Duke of Edinburgh* of the First Cruiser Squadron, occupied a position at the van, and acted as a connecting link between the battle fleet and the battle-cruiser fleet.

This squadron, although it carried out useful work, did not have an opportunity of coming into action.

The Fourth Light-cruiser Squadron, under Commodore Charles E. Le Mesurier, occupied a position in the van until ordered to attack enemy destroyers at 7.20 p.m., and again at 8.18 p.m., when they supported the Eleventh Flotilla, which had moved out under Commodore James R.P. Hawksley, to attack.

On each occasion the Fourth Light-cruiser Squadron was very well handled by Commodore Le Mesurier, his captains giving him excellent support, and their object was attained, although with some loss in the second attack, when the ships came under the heavy fire of the enemy battle fleet at between 6,500 and 8,000 yards.

The *Calliope* was hit several times, but did not sustain serious damage, although, I regret to say, she had several casualties. The light-cruisers attacked the enemy's battleships with torpedoes at this time, and an explosion on board a ship of the Kaiser class was seen at 8.40 p.m.

During these destroyer attacks four enemy torpedo-boat destroyers were sunk by the gunfire of battleships, lightcruisers and destroyers.

After the arrival of the British Battle Fleet the enemy's tactics were of a nature generally to avoid further action, in which they were favoured by the conditions of visibility.

At 9 p.m. the enemy was entirely out of sight, and the threat of torpedo-boat destroyer attacks during the rapidly approaching darkness made it necessary for me to dispose the fleet for the night, with a view to its safety from such attacks, whilst providing for a renewal of action at daylight.

I accordingly manoeuvred to remain between the enemy and his bases, placing our flotillas in a position in which they would afford protection to the fleet from destroyer attack, and at the same time be favourably situated for attacking the enemy's heavy ships.

During the night the British heavy ships were not attacked, but the Fourth, Eleventh and Twelfth Flotillas, under Commodore Hawksley and Captains Charles J. Wintour and Anselan J.B. Stirling, delivered a series of very gallant and successful attacks on the enemy, causing him heavy losses.

It was during these attacks that severe losses in the Fourth Flotilla occurred, including that of *Tipperary*, with the gallant leader of the Flotilla, Captain Wintour. He had brought his flotilla to a high pitch of perfection, and although suffering severely from the fire of the enemy, a heavy toll of enemy vessels was taken, and many gallant actions were performed by the flotilla.

Two torpedoes were seen to take effect on enemy vessels as the result of the attacks of the Fourth Flotilla, one being from *Spitfire*, and the other from either *Ardent*, *Ambuscade* or *Garland*.

The attack carried out by the Twelfth Flotilla (Captain Anselan J.B. Stirling) was admirably executed. The squadron attack, which consisted of six large vessels, besides light-cruisers, and comprised vessels of the *Kaiser* class, was taken by surprise.

A large number of torpedoes was fired, including some at the second and third ships in the line; those fired at the third ship took effect, and she was observed to blow up. A second attack made twenty minutes later by *Maenad* on the five vessels still remaining, resulted in the fourth ship in the line being also hit.

The destroyers were under a heavy fire from the light-cruisers on reaching the rear of the line, but the *Onslaught* was the only vessel which received any material injuries.

During the attack carried out by the Eleventh Flotilla, Castor (Commodore James R.P. Hawksley) leading the flotilla, engaged and sank an enemy torpedo-boat destroyer at point-blank range.

There were many gallant deeds performed by the destroyer flotillas; they surpassed the very highest expectations that I had formed of them.

Apart from the proceedings of the flotillas, the Second Light-cruiser Squadron in the rear of the battle fleet was in close action for about 15 minutes at 10.20 p.m. with a squadron comprising one enemy cruiser and four light-cruisers, during which period *Southampton* and *Dublin* suffered rather heavy casualties, although their steaming and fighting qualities were not impaired. The return fire of the squadron appeared to be very effective.

Abdiel, ably commanded by Commander Berwick Curtis, carried out her duties with the success which has always characterized her work.

At daylight, June 1st, the battle fleet, being then to the southward and westward of the Horn Reef, turned to the northward in search of enemy vessels and for the purpose of collecting our own cruisers and torpedo-boat destroyers.

At 2.30 a.m. Vice-Admiral Sir Cecil Burney

transferred his flag from *Marlborough* to *Revenge*, as the former ship had some difficulty in keeping up the speed of the squadron. *Marlborough* was detached by my direction to a base, successfully driving off an enemy submarine attack en route.

The visibility early on June 1st (three to four miles) was less than on May 31st, and the torpedo-boat destroyers, being out of visual touch, did not rejoin until 9 a.m.

The British Fleet remained in the proximity of the battlefield and near the line of approach to German ports until 11 a.m. on June 1st, in spite of the disadvantage of long distances from fleet bases and the danger incurred in waters adjacent to enemy coasts from submarines and torpedo craft.

The enemy, however, made no sign, and I was reluctantly compelled to the conclusion that the High Sea Fleet had returned into port.

Subsequent events proved this assumption to have been correct. Our position must have been known to the enemy, as at 4 a.m. the Fleet engaged a Zeppelin for about five minutes, during which time she had ample opportunity to note and subsequently report the position and course of the British Fleet.

The waters from the latitude of the Horn Reef to the scene of the action were thoroughly searched, and some survivors from the destroyers *Ardent*, *Fortune* and *Tipperary* were picked up, and the *Sparrowhawk*, which had been in collision and was no longer seaworthy, was sunk after her crew had been taken off.

A large amount of wreckage was seen, but no enemy ships, and at 1.15 p.m., it being evident that the German Fleet had succeeded in returning to port, course was shaped for our bases, which were reached without further incident on Friday, June 2nd.

A cruiser squadron was detached to search for *Warrior*, which vessel had been abandoned whilst in tow of *Engadine* on her way to the base owing to bad weather setting in and the vessel becoming unseaworthy, but no trace of her was discovered, and a further subsequent search by a light-cruiser squadron having failed to locate her, it is evident that she foundered.

The enemy fought with the gallantry that was expected of him. We particularly admired the conduct of those on board a disabled German light-cruiser which passed down the British line shortly after deployment, under a heavy fire, which was returned by the only gun left in action.

The conduct of officers and men throughout the day and night actions was entirely beyond praise. No words of mine could do them justice. On all sides it is reported to me that the glorious traditions of the past were most worthily upheld – whether in heavy ships, cruisers, light-cruisers, or destroyers – the same admirable spirit prevailed.

Officers and men were cool and determined, with a cheeriness that would have carried them through anything. The heroism of the wounded was the admiration of all.

I cannot adequately express the pride with which the spirit of the Fleet filled me.

Bibliography and further reading

Official Admiralty and Royal Navy primary source documents

Bacon, Captain R.C. *Report on the Experimental Cruise* (1907).

Director of Naval Ordnance, Considerations of the Design of a Battleship (1906).

'Fire Control and Secondary Armament (an answer to the complaint that the *Dreadnought* has insufficient secondary armament)' (July 1906).

'HMS *Dreadnought* – Plans of Decks' (1906).

'HMS *Dreadnought* (Notes for Use of the Parliamentary Secretary in Debate' (June 1906).

'Memorandum Explanatory of the Programme of New Construction for 1905–1906, with Details Omitted from the Navy Estimates for 1906–1907' (1906).

Naval Controller, 'Comparison of various Guns for Secondary Armament of Battleships' (n.d.).

Naval Intelligence Division, 'HM ships *Dreadnought* and *Invincible*: memorandum' (n.d.).

'Naval Strength of Principal Maritime Powers showing in detail Dreadnoughts built, building and projected' (1908).

'The Balance of Naval Power' (1906).

'Turning Powers of the Dreadnought' (1906).

Slade, Captain E.J.W., 'Lecture on Speed in Battleships' (n.d.).

St Erme Cardew, John, Journal kept by John St Erme Cardew as Midshipman on HMS *Dreadnought* 15 September 1909–7 September 1910.

Books

Allen, Richard W., *Air Supply to Boiler Rooms of Modern Ships of War* (London, Charles Griffin & Co., 1921).

Breyer, Siegfried, *Battleships and Battle Cruisers, 1905–1970*, trans. by Alfred Kurti (London, MacDonald & Jane's, 1973).

Brown, David K., *The Grand Fleet: Warship Design and Development 1906–1922* (Barnsley, Seaforth, 1997).

Burr, Lawrence, *British Battlecruisers 1914–18* (Oxford, Osprey, 2006).

Burt, R.A., *British Battleships of World War One* (Barnsley, Seaforth, 2012).

Buxton, Ian and Johnston, Ian, *The Battleship Builders: Constructing and Arming British Capital Ships* (Barnsley, Seaforth, 2013).

Chant, Christopher, *Twentieth-Century War Machines – Sea* (London, Chancellor Press, 1999).

Draminski, Stefan, *The Battleship HMS Dreadnought (Super drawings in 3D)* (Lublin, Kagero, 2013).

Friedman, Norman, *Naval Firepower: Battleship Guns and Gunnery in the Dreadnought Era* (Barnsley, Seaforth, 2008).

Friedman, Norman, *Naval Weapons of World War One: Guns, Torpedoes, Mines and ASW Weapons of all Nations – An Illustrated Directory* (Barnsley, Seaforth, 2011).

Golding, Harry (ed.), *The Wonder Book of Ships* (London, Ward, Lock & Co., n.d.).

Golding, Harry (ed.), *The Wonder Book of the Navy* (London, Ward, Lock & Co. n.d.).

Hodges, Peter, *The Big Gun: Battleship Main Armament 1860–1945* (London, Conway Maritime Press, 1981).

Hough, Richard, *Dreadnought: A History of the Modern Battleship* (London, Endeavour Press, 2015).

Hythe, Viscount (ed.), *The Naval Annual 1913* (Portsmouth, J. Griffin & Co., 1913).

Jane's Fighting Ships of World War I (London, Studio Editions, 1990).

Keegan, John, *Battle at Sea* (London, Pimlico, 1993).

Konstam, Angus, *British Battleships 1914–18 (1): The Early Dreadnoughts* (Oxford, Osprey, 2013).

Konstam, Angus, *British Battleships 1914–18 (2): The Super Dreadnoughts* (Oxford, Osprey, 2013).

Leather, John, *World Warships in Review 1860–1906* (London, Purnell, 1976).

Parkinson, Roger, *Dreadnought – The Ship that Changed the World* (London, I.B. Tauris, 2015).

Roberts, John, *The Battleship Dreadnought – Anatomy of the Ship* (London, Conway, 2013).

Thomas, Roger D. and Patterson, Brian, *Dreadnoughts in Camera* (Stroud, Sutton, 1998).

Index